HOMOSEXUALITY AND THE LAW

This volume is published in hardback as Volume I of the monograph series, *Research on Homosexuality*.

Series Editor: John P. De Cecco, Ph.D., Director, Center for Homosexual Education, Evaluation & Research (C.H.E.E.R.), San Francisco State University, and Editor, *Journal of Homosexuality*. Volumes in this series include:

Volume 1: *Homosexuality & the Law*
(The hardbound edition of Volume 5, Nos. 1-2 of the *Journal of Homosexuality*. **Guest Editor. Donald C. Knutson, J.D.**) Fall-Winter 1979/80.

Volume 2: *Homosexuality & History*
(The hardbound edition of Volume 6, Nos. 1-2 of the *Journal of Homosexuality*. Guest Co-editors: Sal Licata, Ph.D. and **Bob Peterson, Ph.D. Cand.**) **Fall 1980.**

Volume 3: *Homosexuality & Sexually Transmitted Diseases*
Edited by David G. Ostrow. M.D., Ph. D. and Terry Alan Sandholzer. Fall 1980.

forthcoming volumes:
Homosexuality & Psychotherapy
Homosexuality & Substance Abuse
Homosexuality & The Philosophy of Science

This series is published by The Haworth Press, Inc., under the editorial auspices of the Center for Homosexual Education, Evaluation & Research (C.H.E.E.R), San Francisco State University, and the *Journal of Homosexuality*.

HOMOSEXUALITY
AND
THE LAW

A special double issue of the *Journal of Homosexuality*
(Fall 1979-Winter 1980), Volume 5, Nos. 1 and 2

Guest Editor: Donald C. Knutson, J.D.

ISBN: 0–917724-14-3, Cloth cover
ISBN: 0–917724-15-1, Paper cover
ISSN: 0001 8369

The Haworth Press, 149 Fifth Avenue, New York, New York 10010

Library of Congress Cataloging in Publication Data
Main entry under title:

Homosexuality and the law.

  (Research on homosexuality ; v. 1)
  Special issue of Journal of homosexuality, v. 5, no.
1/2.
  Includes bibliographical references.
  1. Homosexuals--Legal status, laws, etc.--United
States--Addresses, essays, lectures. I. Knutson,
Donald C. II. Journal of homosexuality. III. Series.
KF4754.5.H65   342'.73'085   79-23673
ISBN 0-917724-14-3

Printed in the United States of America.

TO

Richard Rouilard

and

Howard Teich

The *Journal of Homosexuality* is devoted to empirical research, and its clinical implications, on lesbianism, male homosexuality, gender identity, and alternative sexual lifestyles. It was created to serve the allied professional groups represented by psychology, sociology, anthropology, medicine, and law. Its purposes are:

a) to bring together, within one contemporary periodical, rigorous empirical research on homosexuality and gender identity;

b) to provide scholarly research which, although not rooted in strict experimental methodology, has heuristic value for the understanding of homosexuality and gender identity;

c) to show the implications of these findings for helping professionals in a wide variety of disciplines and settings.

MANUSCRIPTS. Manuscripts may be submitted to John P. De Cecco, Editor, *Journal of Homosexuality,* Center for Homosexual Education, Evaluation and Research, San Francisco State University, San Francisco, California 94132. Information concerning the preparation of manuscripts may be obtained from the Editor.

The *Journal of Homosexuality* is published quarterly in Fall, Winter, Spring, and Summer. Volume One was published over a two-year period: Vol. 1(1), Fall 1974; Vol. 1(2), Winter 1975–76; Vol. 1(3), Spring 1976; Vol. 1(4), Summer 1976.

BUSINESS OFFICE. All subscription and advertising inquiries should be directed to The Haworth Press, 149 Fifth Avenue, New York, New York 10010. Telephone (212)228-2800.

SUBSCRIPTIONS. Subscriptions are on an academic year, per-volume basis only. Payment must be made in U.S. funds only. For Canadian orders, add $5.00; other foreign orders, add $10.00. Prices:

Libraries: $45.00, (Please note The Haworth Press, Inc. extends to all library subscribers the right to make unlimited photocopying for noncommerical, patron use or, until further notice, network and resource-sharing programs, including inter-library loan. No further permission is necessary or required, and no per-copy fee is charged. Librarians may also make multiple photocopies for reserve room use or for student distribution with no fees or permissions required.)

Institutions: $42.00. (Price applicable to academic departments, social agencies, foundations, government agencies, corporations, hospitals, and all other institutions where payment or invoice recipient is institutional in nature.)

Individuals: $24.00. (Price applicable as a professional discount, where payment is made by personal check only.) The above tier-pricing policy of The Haworth Press, Inc. is intended to distribute the rising costs of publication differentially according to the use of periodical literature.

INDEX. An annual index to authors and subjects is included in the Summer issue of each volume of the *Journal of Homosexuality.*

In addition, articles from the *Journal of Homosexuality* are selectively indexed or abstracted in the *ABS Guide to the Behavioral and Social Sciences, Abstracts for Social Workers, Abstracts in Anthropology, BioSciences Information Service of Biological Abstracts (BIOSIS), Le Bullétin Signaletique, Chicago Psychoanalytic Literature Index, College Student Personnel Abstracts, Criminal Justice Abstracts, Current Contents: Behavioral and Social Sciences, Excerpta Medica, Index Medicus, Index to Periodical Articles Related to Law, Pastoral Care and Counseling Abstracts, Selected List of Tables of Contents of Psychiatric Periodicals, Psychological Abstracts, Psychological Reader's Guide, Social Science Citation Index, Sociological Abstracts,* and *Women's Studies Abstracts.*

Selected articles are also cited through *CERDIC* (France), *ERIC/CAPS, International Bibliography of the Social Sciences,* and the *National Criminal Justice Reference Service (NCJRS) Index.*

CHANGE OF ADDRESS. Please notify the Subscription Department. The Haworth Press, 149 Fifth Avenue, New York, New York 10010 of address change. Please allow six weeks for processing; *include old and new addresses,* including zip codes.

Library of Congress Catalog Card Number: 74-78295

Second-class postage paid at New York, New York, and at additional mailing offices.

JOURNAL OF HOMOSEXUALITY

HOMOSEXUALITY & THE LAW

A SPECIAL DOUBLE ISSUE OF
THE JOURNAL OF HOMOSEXUALITY

Compiled and Edited by Donald C. Knutson

Volume 5, Numbers 1/2, Fall-Winter 1979/80

FOREWORD

This special issue of the *Journal of Homosexuality* inaugurates the new publication plans of the current editorship, developed conjointly with The Haworth Press and the Center for Homosexual Education, Evaluation and Research (C.H.E.E.R.). These plans involve the publication of special issues of the *Journal* devoted to single themes and disciplines and the publication of scholarly volumes devoted to research on various aspects of homosexuality. In some cases, the special *Journal* issues will also be published as single volumes. Plans are well underway for special issues or volumes for the following: clinical aspects of sexually transmitted disease, social and political issues in providing health care for homosexual men and women, history of homosexuality, and psychotherapy. Plans for special issues in the arts and humanities are also under discussion. Suggestions for other special issues or volumes are most welcome.

The theme for the first symposium, to be published in two consecutive issues (under one binding) is homosexuality and the law. The purpose of the symposium is to show how the law as viewed and decided by the courts often embodies fear and prejudice against homosexuality and, thereby, becomes the instrument for discrimination. This double-issue of the *Journal* will also be published as the first volume in the research series.

Professor Knutson, the guest editor of the symposium, has led the law profession in the study of the judicial interpretation of the rights of homosexual men and women. With the help of other law professors and practicing lawyers, he has assembled a series of articles that address important legal issues arising out of the homosexuality of American citizens.

On behalf of the editorial staff of the *Journal*, I wish to express my deep appreciation to Professor Knutson and his fellow contributors for undertaking the task of illuminating the relationship of the law to homosexuality. I also express my appreciation to Stuart Kellogg, the manuscript editor of the *Journal,* for his patient, skilled midwifing and editing of each piece in the symposium.

John P. De Cecco, Ph.D.
Editor

About The Editor

Donald C. Knutson is Professor of Law at the University of Southern California; Executive Director, Gay Rights Advocates, a public interest law firm in San Francisco; and legal counsel to the Center for Homosexual Education. Evaluation and Research. The editor wishes to express his gratitude to Stuart Kellogg for invaluable assistance in compiling and editing these essays.

INTRODUCTION

Donald C. Knutson, J.D.

Sex is a pale, undernourished part of self for most Americans. We live in a culture that is phobic in its fear of and obsessive attention to sex. We have learned to feel most comfortable when the sexual aspects of self develop in darkened areas of our being where the light of awareness, understanding, and acceptance rarely penetrates. And of this neglected and distorted part of self called sex, those facets that might be called homosexual are the most carefully hidden.[1]

Decisions concerning sexual issues belong to the least distinguished chapters of American jurisprudence. Consider the unseemly judicial wrangling[2] in the apparently unending series of cases that have attempted to assess free speech values in obscenity disputes. The failure of the judicial system to deal rationally with the problem of obscenity can be explained by society's fear of sex, a phobia internalized by much of the judiciary. I know of no more dramatic illustration of institutionalized obsession with sex, however, than the myriad of statues, policies, regulations, and judicial decisions that provide this country with the most fervently anti-homosexual laws in the Western World.

Until very recently, such laws, no matter how draconian, went virtually unchallenged. It was simply taken for granted that government was free to impose whatever measures thought necessary in its relentless, yet obviously futile, effort to stamp out homosexuality. The last decade, however, has witnessed a remarkable surge of litigation challenging these laws and policies as arbitrary and discriminatory excesses of governmental power. The response of the American judicial system has been uneven, at best. Published opinions reflect virulent and open hostility.[3] It would seem that judges were searching for *any* rationalization, plausible or not, to justify governmental discrimination.[4] Not only are the cases inconsistent in result, they fail to provide a rational framework or even some common doctrinal basis for the resolution of these difficult and important issues.

This special edition of the *Journal of Homosexuality* is devoted to a comprehensive study of those decisions. The essays cover a wide range of subjects, illustrating the extent to which the lives of gay persons are touched by these laws and providing a highly critical examination of the response by the American judicial system to our claims for equal protection under the law. The authors of these essays are in substantial agree ment that: (a) the law and the legal process, which may either mandate discriminatory practices[5] or permit discrimination to occur without legal redress,[6] seriously impinge upon the constitutional liberties of more than a million Americans; (b) the disarray in the decisional law results principally from the differing perceptions and visceral reactions of individual judges with respect to the phenomenon of homosexuality; and (c) the refusal of the United States Supreme Court to provide guidance or leadership fosters and exacerbates the problem.

In the opening essay, "The Legal Arena — Progress for Gay Civil Rights," Professor Vetri discusses two books that have attempted to disentangle the confusion. He cautions that intellectual argument or appeals to evidence are unlikely to persuade persons, including judges, whose attitudes toward homosexuality are basically irrational. Yet Vetri is optimistic for the future, arguing that public attitudes toward homosexuality are changing and that "grand constitutional decisions" have typically followed, rather than preceded, evolving public mores. The plethora of unprincipled and contradictory decisions that continues to represent the majority view is explained by persistent adherence to several theories reflective of the mythology surrounding homosexuality, a mythology so totally unsupported by fact it calls into question the courts' own standards of rationality. Predominant among these rationales is the "criminality" theory, which holds that the existence of laws proscribing the act of sodomy establishes the criminal status of all persons who can be labelled "homosexual," which, in turn, justifies refusal to provide constitutional protections. Although the sodomy laws have traditionally applied to heterosexual as well as homosexual conduct, in the prevailing view homosexuality is considered "a sexual life style that contemplates routine violation" of the law.[7]

A recent case in point is *Gay Lib* v. *University of Missouri,*[8] which involved a broad constitutional challenge to the refusal by the University of Missouri to grant official recognition to a gay student organization. Despite recommendations for approval from the appropriate student and faculty committees, the University administration rejected Gay Lib's application because of "a concern for the impact of recognition on the general relationship of the University to the public at large."[9] A civil rights action was then filed, alleging that the University's refusal to recognize Gay Lib infringed the students' First Amendment guarantee of freedom of association and denied them equal protection of the laws. The federal district court judge held that those constitutional protections need not be extended to members of Gay Lib, reasoning that "that association is likely to incite, promote, and result in acts contrary to and in violation of the sodomy statute." The "evidence" that supported this conclusion was provided by Dr. Charles Socarides, a psychiatrist, who testified that "whenever you have a convocation of homosexuals, that you are going to have increased homosexual activities, which, of course, includes sodomy

. . . so that any gathering would certainly promote such illegal sexual conduct."[10]

The criminality theory played a decisive role in *Gaylord* v. *Tacoma School District,* where the majority opinion held that "homosexuality connotes illegal acts, because sexual gratification with a member of one's own sex is *implicit* in the term 'homosexual'."[11] Although there was no evidence that Mr. Gaylord had engaged in sexual acts of *any* kind, much less any proof that he had violated Washington's repealed sodomy laws,[12] the court held that his acknowledgment of "his status as a homosexual" made it "unquestioned" that he had violated the law. Thus, although "there was *uncontroverted evidence* that he was a competent and intelligent teacher,"[13] his dismissal was justified by the assumption that he was a criminal.

The geneology of the sodomy laws is examined in detail in Professor Oaks' chapter, "Perceptions of Homosexuality by Justices of the Peace in Colonial Virginia." Oaks explains that the present laws were derived from Henry VIII's buggery statute of 1533,[14] a law apparently more important to the King as a blow to ecclesiastical privilege than as a means of suppressing vice. The English statute was transplanted to America, almost verbatim, early in our colonial history. Oaks indicates that the continuing pattern of strict anti-homosexual statutes and provisions for harsh sentencing (including the penalty of "death without benefit of Clergy")[15] proves that fear of sodomy flourished independently of actual experience, for colonial authors were eager to insist on the rarity of homosexual behavior. The existence of sodomy laws appears to have bolstered anti-homosexual prejudices that might otherwise have atrophied.

These biases, perceived by modern judges as reflective of societal attitudes, pervade their decisions. Published opinions express open distaste for homosexuality, which is commonly described as "loathsome and disgusting";[16] "grossly repugnant";[17] "degenerate";[18] "anathema";[19] "inherently abhorrent";[20] "foul";[21] and "unfit to be named among Christians."[22] It is hardly surprising then, that such courts routinely sanction the denial of civil rights to those they assume to be "homosexual."

Another rationale for discrimination is based on the notion that homosexuality is "unnatural" or "abnormal," which somehow justifies criminalization of homosexual conduct and, by some courts, authorizes governmental proscription of the status of homosexuality. This theory is rooted, no doubt, in traditional proscription by the sodomy laws of "The Crime Against Nature" with no further definition of the conduct intended to be prohibited. The fact that the phrase "crime against nature" is hardly self-explanatory has resulted in an inordinate amount of litigation where courts have wrestled with such momentous problems as whether cunnilingus,[23] oral copulation,[24] masturbation,[25] or other common sexual practices fell within the proscription of the statute. Not surprisingly, when inquiry is confined to a linguistic search for the "natural," there has been little agreement on the sweep of these laws.

Some courts seem intuitively to know what is "unnatural." Pressed to demonstrate the unnaturalness of fellatio, for example, the Supreme Court of Oklahoma responded that "it is *self-evident* that the use of the alimentary canal for the purpose of sexual copulation is against the natural design of the human body." Thus, as an offense against nature, it was perfectly proper for the state to criminalize the act.[26]

The ambiguity of the term "crime against nature" has been the basis of numerous claims, most of which have been rejected, that the law is unconstitutionally vague. As one constitutional scholar put it: "If that language did not appear among the sex offenses in the penal code and did not carry such a stiff penalty, one might think that its purpose is to keep people from walking horses on the grass."[27] The response by the Supreme Court of Louisiana to claims of unconstitutional vagueness is typically circular:[28]

These words [the crime against nature] have a well-defined, well understood, and generally accepted meaning, i.e., any carnal copulation or sexual joining that is devious and abnormal *because it does not conform to the order obtained by nature.*

The difficulties entailed in any responsible attempt to determine what is or is not "unnatural" conduct and, once that conclusion has been reached, to decide why governmental sanctions may be appropriate, are addressed by Professor Richards in his essay, "Homosexual Acts and the Constitutional Right to Privacy." Richards asserts that the term "unnatural" implies a proper function gone awry. The term was apparently first applied in literature to male homosexuality by Plato who, with the confident sexism of his day, identified homosexuality as degrading men to what he perceived as the ignoble status of women and as frustrating the only "natural" purpose of sex: i.e., procreation. By way of St. Augustine, St. Thomas Aquinas and Sir William Blackstone, the notion that homosexuality violates an established order of nature entered American law.

Contradicting this view, Richards argues that this attempt to restrict sexual activity exclusively to the purpose of procreation is itself "unnatural," since human beings obviously have the capacity to direct their sexuality to the expression of romantic love and to recreation as well as to procreation. He asserts in the terminology of contractarian moral theory that the individual's liberty to love in any way that truly contributes to self-respect is a "general good" that must be lightly trespassed upon by the majority. Richards recognizes individual autonomy — "the right to be left alone" — as the fundamental civil liberty on which the constitutional right of privacy, developed in recent court decisions dealing with contraception and abortion, was based.

Obviously, there is no evidence, empirical or otherwise, that homosexuality is unnatural.[29] Delvin and other opponents of the tolerant Wolfenden Report had to rely on the ordinary citizen's unpredictable and unscientific *intuition* of right and wrong to "prove" that homosexuality is against the order of nature and, therefore, should remain illegal.[30] Unfortunately, too many modern courts continued to trumpet this theme.

Conventional wisdom has it that an appropriate function of government is to "protect and improve the moral tone of society." From this it is argued that once a person, or a class of persons, is labelled "immoral," governmental discrimination is constitutionally justifiable. In the recent political campaigns to repeal ordinances protecting gay persons from discrimination, it was often asserted that "anyone who is immoral is a second-class citizen" and unworthy of civil rights.[31] But how does a court, once it is willing to subscribe to that view, then decide whether or not particular behaviors or classes of persons are "immoral"? A typical response is that of the United States Court of Claims, which proclaimed that:[32]

Any schoolboy knows *that a homosexual act is immoral, indecent, lewd and obscene.*

Although our political system purports to sharply demarcate religious dogma from governmental policy, many courts rely unhesitatingly on the Old Testament and on other Judeo-Christian religious works to "prove" that homosexuality is "immoral" and therefore subject to governmental stricture. In the *Gaylord* case, for example, the question was a simple one: whether a schoolteacher could lawfully be discharged solely because he was a "known homosexual." The court posed the determinative issue as:[33]

"Was Gaylord guilty of immorality?"

The court recognized that "in its abstract sense, the term is not and perhaps cannot be comprehensively defined." Nevertheless, relying on the *New Catholic Encyclopedia,* it found that since "homosexuality is widely condemned as immoral and was so condemned as immoral during biblical times,"[34] Gaylord's admission of being "homosexual" constituted an admission of being "immoral" and justified his dismissal.

In *Dew* v. *Halaby*[35] an Air Force veteran with an unimpeached work record was dismissed from his position as air traffic controller because he admitted to having "committed at least four unnatural sex acts with males," when he was eighteen years old. Although it was conceded that these acts "had no relation to his competency and ability to perform the duties of his position," the judge found that "common sense" dictates that government must have the power to discharge persons who have engaged in "immoral" acts. Dismissal was appropriate because:[36]

To require employees to work with persons who have committed acts which are repugnant to the established and accepted standards of decency and morality can only have a disrupting effect upon the morals and efficiency of any organization.

The development of legal theory responsive to claims that the "immorality" of the homosexual orientation is a permissible criterion for prohibiting access to employment opportunities is examined by Judith Hedgpeth in "Employment Discrimination Law and the Rights of Gay Persons." She describes early challenges to the Federal Civil Service Regulations, which mandated blanket disqualification of gay persons. These cases were summarily dismissed by courts that equated homosexuality with "immorality" and asserted that "homosexuals are dangerous to the moral fibre of the nation."[37] The early decisions simply assumed that proof of homosexual conduct necessitated termination of any employee, on the theory that continued employment would "bring the government service into public contempt."[38] In 1969, the Court of Appeals for the District of Columbia forcefully rejected that approach:[39]

The notion it could be an appropriate function of the federal bureaucracy to enforce the majority's conventional moral code of conduct in the private lives of its employees is at war with elementary concepts of liberty, privacy and diversity.

That view was not received enthusiastically by other courts. A series of successful challenges followed, however, building on the theme that the homosexuality of an employee cannot, in itself, justify dismissal or restrict opportunities for promotion.[40] The theory that "immorality" could be an appropriate criterion in governmental employment policies was finally discarded in new Regulations promulgated in 1975 in response to a court order to "forthwith cease excluding or discharging from government service any homosexual person" solely because of "unparticularized and unsubstantiated conclusions that possible embarrassment about the employee's homosexual conduct threatens the quality of the government's performance."[41] Theoretically, at any rate, occupational qualifications are now to be the test of eligibility for federal employment, rather than notions about the "morality" of an employee's sexual orientation.

Until the American Psychiatric Association removed "homosexuality" from its official nomenclature of mental disorders,[42] it was commonplace for courts to justify governmental discrimination on the ground that homosexuality is a psychopathic disability that impairs vocational functioning. This so-called "sickness theory" had been used, for example, to justify denial of security clearances to gay applicants, on the ground that:[43]

the lack of emotional stability which is found in most sex perverts and the weakness of their moral fiber, makes them susceptible to the blandishments of the foreign espionage agent.

In *Doe* v. *Department of Transportation,* the court upheld the Federal Aeronautic Administration's denial of the medical certificate necessary to obtain a private pilot's license, holding that the applicant's homosexuality indicated he was "afflicted with a severe personality disorder that endangered the safety not only of the applicant but of the public.[44] There was, of course, no evidence before the court that the applicant was mentally unstable. In fact, a clinical psychologist hired by the government to examine the applicant was unable to diagnose any existing character or behavior disorder. Yet the court "remained unconvinced" that the homosexuality of the applicant should not be determinative of his mental competence.[45]

The notion that the status of homosexuality constitutes a psychological dysfunction was the justification given by a federal court to uphold the military's blanket disqualification of lesbians and gay men:[46]

It would be clearly inappropriate to hobble the Army by forcing it to retain even one soldier when there are serious questions concerning his emotional health.

Another court, anxious to prevent the dishonorable discharge of an "outstanding officer with fourteen years of exceptional service" including forty combat missions in World War II, "assumed" that his "homosexual complications" were due "to trauma caused by repeated air missions in combat" or "to a variant of a preretirement psychiatric syndrome," an assumption that would justify his separation for "physical disability" rather than "homosexuality" and would thereby permit him to escape the stigma of dishonorable discharge.[47]

Perhaps the apogee of the sickness theory was reached in an outlandish decision from New Jersey, *Gish* v. *Board of Education.*[48] Pursuant to a statute permitting school boards to require "psychiatric or physical examinations of any employee, whenever, in the judgment of the board, an employee shows evidence of deviation from normal physical or mental health," the Board of Education ordered Mr. Gish to submit to a psychiatric examination when they learned of his involvement as president of the Gay Activist Alliance. The court rejected his challenge to the Board's action, on the ground that "a teacher's fitness may not be measured solely by his or her ability to perform the teaching function and ignore the fact that the teacher's presence in the classroom might, nevertheless, pose a danger of harm to the students for a reason not related to academic proficiency." The psychiatric examination was a "reasonable requirement" to determine the teacher's "fitness to be in intimate contact with numbers of impressionable, adolescent pupils."[49]

Although it is a popular argument for justifying discriminatory treatment of gay persons, few courts today openly subscribe to the sickness theory. The *Gaylord* case illustrates an explicit rejection of this argument, which, paradoxically, lent support to the court's holding that Gaylord "made a voluntary choice for which he must be held morally responsible."[50] The sickness theory survives however, as the rationale for deportation orders under a federal statute requiring exclusion of aliens "afflicted with psychopathic personality." That term has been held by the United States Supreme Court to include "*all* homosexuals and other sex perverts."[51] This decision has reinforced the peculiar barriers to aliens described by William Reynolds in "The Immigration and Nationality Act and the Rights of Homosexual Aliens." Reynolds explains that although the Immigration Service has discontinued its earlier practice of automatically disqualifying all gay applicants for naturalization, it continues to adhere to the view that all "homosexuals" are "sexual deviates" and, as such, are automatically excludable from admission to the United States. Thus, aliens who gain entry without identification of their sexual orientations cannot later be denied naturalization on the ground that homosexuality in itself proves a lack of "good moral character."[52] Mr. Reynolds concludes that a recent policy change by the Public Health Service should eventually require the Immigration Service to discard the sickness theory altogether, removing psychological jargon from the domain of legal terminology and restoring it to medical application.

The sickness theory has not been confined to the realm of the psychiatric. Some courts have — quite seriously — argued that homosexuality is a contagious disease requiring isolation of those so "afflicted." A United States Senate Report, commissioned during the McCarthy era to inquire into "The Employment of Homosexuals and Other Sex Perverts," concluded ominously that:[53]

One homosexual can pollute a government office.

The notion that homosexuality can somehow rub off on others has been used to restrict employment opportunities as well as to limit the freedom of all gay persons. It is the theory most often advanced by those opposed to gay men and women serving as teachers or police officers. The argument has not been confined to the lower courts. United States Supreme Court Justice William Rhenquist recently asserted that the constitutional question whether a university could properly refuse a gay student organization permission to hold meetings was "akin to whether those suffering from measles have a constitutional right, in violation of quarantine regulations, to associate together and with others who do not presently have measles."[54]

Akin to the sickness theory is the notion that "homosexuals *commonly* are obsessed with their sexual desires, and are *commonly* compulsive in expressing their desires."[55] Courts have justified discrimination on the ground that "homosexuals *might* engage in notorious and flagrant displays of unorthodox sexual behavior or make offensive overtures while on the job."[56] Extrapolating from those profound generalizations, courts have justified dismissals of employees,[57] have upheld governmental restrictions on the right of gay persons to associate in public establishments,[58] and, most shocking perhaps, have approved removal of children from the custody of their homosexual parent.[59]

The indignities suffered by lesbian mothers and gay fathers in their efforts to maintain custody, or even the right to visit their children, are dramatically illustrated in Donna Hitchen's "Social Standards, Legal Standards, and Personal Trauma in Child Custody Cases." Hitchens contends that before courts can be expected to accept the idea that a gay person can be an effective parent, it will be necessary to dispel the shibboleths that have automatically disqualified gay parents in custody disputes: that a child will be sexually abused by the gay parent, or that the child's sexual orientation will be corrupted by the gay parent's lifestyle. Hitchens points out that there is absolutely no evidence of a correlation between sexual orientation and child abuse, nor is there evidence that homosexuality can be learned or is some kind of contagion that warrants quarantine.

While optimistic for the future, Hitchens warns gay parents that to sue for custody or visitation today is to invite an expensive, exhausting and humiliating ordeal. She ends her chapter with an observation shared by all of the authors of this symposium: Judicial decisions apparently will change only after research and education have abolished the mythology surrounding homosexuality and have begun to change the attitudes of society in general. Her optimism appears justified. For the first time a state supreme court has held that the parent's homosexuality cannot in itself justify a denial of custodial rights. The Supreme Court of Michigan this year unanimously reversed a lower court judge who had awarded custody to the father because the mother is lesbian.[60]

The assumption that the status of homosexuality inevitably carries with it an inability to control sexual appetite has been among the most common rationales for the solicitation laws examined in detail by Joseph Bell in "Public Manifestations of Personal Morality: Limitations on the Use of Solicitation Statutes to Control Homosexual Cruising." This argument was stated succinctly in *Inman* v. *City of Miami*, where the court was faced with a constitutional challenge to a Miami ordinance prohibiting liquor licensees from serving "homosexual persons." The court justified the proscription and upheld the constitutionality of the law on the ground that it was necessary in order to "prevent the congregation at liquor establishments of persons *likely to prey upon the public* by attempting to recruit other persons for acts which have been declared illegal by the Legislature."[61]

Bell effectively demonstrates that the hypothesis, implicit in the solicitation laws, that gay men are bent on "recruiting" unwilling and helpless heterosexual victims is utter nonsense. The solicitation laws, as shown in an important study by the U.C.L.A. *Law Review,* are applied almost exclusively to situations where a decoy policeman has invited an approach in an atmosphere both he and his target understand to be conducive to sexual conduct.[62] Bell demonstrates the constitutional infirmities of these laws, which are especially vulnerable in those states that have decriminalized private sexual conduct between consenting adults. In California, for example, an invitation to engage in perfectly lawful sexual conduct is itself an unlawful act that carries severe penalties, including registration as a "sex offender."[63]

It now appears settled that the federal government, in its role as employer, cannot discriminate on the basis of sexual orientation.[64] Why, then, should the military be free to continue to do so? Because, argued the Attorney General in a recent case:[65]

Tensions and hostilities would certainly exist between known homosexuals and the great majority of naval personnel who despise/detest homosexuality.

The argument that discrimination against a minority is justified by intolerance and prejudice of the majority is not novel. It has been used in support of the miscegenation statutes;[66] to justify removal of the children of interracial marriages;[67] and by the military in its unsuccessful attempt to resist racial integration:[68]

Integration would lower morale and impair efficiency. Whites just will not serve with blacks. The Army must take the country as it is . . . [We are] not an instrument for social experimentation.

This reasoning has firmly established itself in custody cases, where courts commonly hold that the "inevitable" stigmatization of the child of a homosexual parent justifies removal of that child from the home.[69] Although he recognized that "there are problems inherent in burdening a class of people because of the reactions they may engender," the trial judge in *Berg* v. *Clayton* accepted the argument as constitutionally sufficient justification for the Navy's policy that "members involved in homosexuality are military liabilities who cannot be tolerated in a military organization."[70]

Jerel McCrary and Lewis Gutierrez explore the historical attitudes of the government in "The Homosexual Person in the Military and in National Security Employment." While advocates of exclusion from the armed forces have focused on the disruption they assert would otherwise ensue, the security clearance cases have relied more heavily on the "possible subjection to sinister pressures and influences which have traditionally been the lot of homosexuals."[71]

The authors conclude that "perhaps in no other area of gay rights law has progress been so perceptible," but observe that no substantial progress can be expected in this area until gay people receive statutory or judicial protection as a class. It is paradoxical, to say the least, that a judicial system which relies on society's "widespread and deeply rooted revulsion against homosexuality"[72] to justify anti-homosexual laws can, at the same time, find its allure such that "abandonment of the ancient sanction" would lead to "increasing defections from heterosexual behavior and traditional family life."[73]

The concluding essay in this collection, Donald Solomon's "The Emergence of Associational Rights of Homosexual Persons," describes the development of constitutional theory in a series of cases ranging from the right of a state to revoke the license of a gay bar as a "resort for sexual perverts" to the obligation of a state university to grant recognition to a gay student organization. Solomon is highly critical of the role that the U.S. Supreme Court has played, characterizing its inaction as constitutional decision-making "behind an intellectual screen."

Much has been made of the high Court's summary affirmance of *Doe* v. *Commonwealth*,[74] where a divided three-judge federal court in Virginia declined in 1975 to grant declaratory or injunctive relief to bar enforcement of the state's criminal sodomy statute. That action, coupled with the Court's consistent denial of certiorari in cases where the constitutional claims of gay persons have been raised, has been viewed by many as ominous.

Theoretically, at any rate, such dispositions are not to be taken as indicative of the Court's views on the merits of the claims presented. Nevertheless, some courts and many commentators have understandably construed the Court's refusal to give its views on the extent to which the Constitution may limit state regulation of private sexual conduct as a judgment that gay persons are entitled to no constitutional protection from laws that restrict our private sexual conduct or consign us to the status of criminals, and that government is free to limit our access to housing, public accommodations, and employment opportunities. Solomon characterizes as "unprincipled" the view that judicial deference to other branches of government requires the Court "to avoid embroiling [itself] in this controversial area of social policy."[75] He predicts that guidance and leadership by the Court is "essential to developing a concept of homosexual persons as a class worthy to enjoy constitutional protections."

Mr. Solomon's point is illustrated by the strikingly contradictory dispositions of two essentially identical lawsuits that had been filed in San Francisco several years ago to challenge the Pacific Telephone and Telegraph Company's policy of refusing employment opportunities to "manifest homosexuals." The state case, *Gay Law Students Association* v. *Pacific Tel. & Tel.*,[76] named the California Fair Employment Practice Commission as a co-defendent. The federal counterpart, The Equal Employment Opportunity Commission, was joined as a defendant in the companion federal case, *De Santis* v. *Pacific Tel. & Tel.*[77] Motions to dismiss the complaints were granted by both trial judges, and appeals were eventually perfected to the California Supreme Court and the United States Court of Appeals for the Ninth Circuit. Coincidentally, decisions in both appeals were announced on the same day, May 31, 1979.

The EEOC and the FEPC had consistently refused to hear claims of discrimination based on sexual orientation. Both Commissions argued that legislation providing redress for discrimination based on "sex"[78] was intended to apply exclusively to gender-based discrimination — "to ensure that men and women are treated equally"[79] — and, therefore, did not include "sexual preference such as homosexuality." Rejection by the Congress and the California Legislature of efforts to amend these statutes to include sexual orientation was taken as determinative of the legislative intent of both bodies.

On this issue, the appellate courts agreed. In a 2-to-1 decision, the Ninth Circuit held that dismissal of the complaint against the EEOC was proper, since judicial construction of the statute to include "protection for homosexuals" would "frustrate Congressional objectives" and "violate the rule that our duty . . . is to ascertain and give effect to the legislative will." The California Supreme Court agreed, in a unanimous ruling, that the plaintiffs had failed to state a claim against the FEPC. The Court held that no constitutional principle prevents reform "one step at a time," or requires that the Legislature "strike all evils at the same time."

It was the issue of PT&T's liability for its alleged discriminatory policy that led the two courts to disagree. In *De Santis,* the plaintiffs had based their claims against PT&T on section 1985(3) of the Federal Civil Rights Act, which forbids conspiracies to deprive "any person or class of persons of the equal protection of the laws." The Ninth Circuit perceived the determinative question to be whether "homosexuals, as a class, can claim the special protection of §1985(3)." The Court recognized that the statute "has been liberated from the now anachronistic historical circumstances of reconstruction America," but concluded that "in contradistinction to . . . blacks . . . and women . . . it cannot be said that homosexuals are a suspect or quasi–suspect class" subjecting "such classification" to strict judicial scrutiny under the equal protection clause of the Fourteenth Amendment. The majority opinion chides the plaintiffs for employing "an artifice to 'bootstrap' protection for homosexuals," and holds that the district court properly rejected their claims against PT&T.

The concurring judge agreed: "This section is not a writ by which the judiciary can provide comfort and succor to all groups, large and small, who feel social disapproval from time to time. Like many others, homosexuals do not enjoy section 1985(3) protection." He relied on the United States Supreme Court's summary affirmance of *Doe* v. *Commonwealth*[80] to establish that "homosexuals" are not a class deserving "special federal assistance in protecting their civil rights."

The California Supreme Court, however, in a 4-to-3 decision, reversed the judgment for PT&T in the *Gay Law Students Association* case. The majority opinion found "particularly untenable" PT&T's claim "that it enjoys the power arbitrarily to exclude classes of individuals from its numerous employment opportunities without regard to constitutional constraints," and flatly held that the equal protection clause does not permit the state "to exclude homosexuals as a class from employment opportunities without a showing that the individual's homosexuality renders him unfit for the job from which he has been excluded." Justice Tobriner reasoned that PT&T was subject to this constitutional mandate, even though it is a privately owned utility, because of "the breadth and depth of governmental regulation" of its business practices, and "the substantial monopoly power granted it by the state." Arbitrary foreclosure of employment opportunities, Tobriner declared, "is one of the most deplorable forms of discrimination known to our society" and protection against it "lies close to the heart of the protection against 'second-class citizenship' which the equal protection clause was intended to guarantee."

This decision has important implications for gay rights litigation for several reasons. It is the first time that a court of last resort has applied the equal protection clause to uphold the claims of gay persons as a protected class. Thus, despite the *De Santis* decision, the "heavy burden" required to justify racial or ethnic discrimination is now to be imposed by California state courts on those who discriminate against gay persons. Contrary to the view of the Ninth Circuit, Tobriner holds that "the aim of the struggle for homosexual rights, and the tactics employed, bear a close analogy to the continuing struggle for civil rights waged by blacks, women and other minorities."

Further, the *Gay Law Student Association* decision marks the first time that any court, much less one with the prestigious reputation of the California Supreme Court, has held that sexual orientation discrimination practiced by anyone other than the federal or state government is constitutionally forbidden. The opinion leaves open the possibility for redress against any discriminating employer who enjoys substantial market power or who can be characterized as a "public service enterprise," such as professional and business associations, unions, newspapers, universities, broadcast media, and hospitals.

Most remarkable, perhaps, is the holding that PT&T's discriminatory policy, if proven, also violated the plaintiffs' political freedom. Relying on a California statute protecting "the fundamental rights of employees in general to engage in political activity without interference by employers," the Court held that acknowledgment of one's homosexuality is a political act. While other courts have viewed coming out as "flaunting" one's homosexuality, an act that provides legal justification for the termination of employment,[81] Tobriner views it differently: "[T]he struggle of the homosexual community for equal rights, particularly in the field of employment, must be recognized as political activity . . . A principal barrier to homosexual equality is the common feeling that homosexuality is an affliction which the homosexual worker must conceal from his employer and his fellow workers. Consequently, one important aspect of the struggle for equal rights is to induce homosexual individuals to 'come out of the closet', acknowledge their sexual preference, and to associate with others in working for equal rights." Since the plaintiffs had alleged that PT&T discriminates "in particular against persons who identify themselves as homosexual, who defend homosexuality, or who are identified with activist homosexual organizations," the Court upheld their right to "maintain a cause of action to recover damages sustained as a result of the employer's unlawful conduct." It is clear that this statute applies to *all* employers, public or private. Thus, the decision protects the employment opportunities of gay Californians who openly acknowledge their lifestyles.

This decision has, of course, no binding application outside California. But the California Supreme Court is one whose opinions are highly regarded, and often followed, by other courts. The opinion will be a tool of inestimable value to lawyers all across the country who are seeking to convince judges that we are a "discrete and insular" minority worthy of and entitled to equality under the law.

Hopefully, this series of essays will encourage dialogue among professionals that will help to dispel the notion that the worth of individual men and women can be determined by stereotypical conduct attributed to "homosexuals." Although theories abound, we know very little of the etiology of homosexuality—or heterosexuality, for that matter. We do know, however, that there are literally millions of persons, myself included, whose sexual and affectional orientation has caused our society to lable us "perverts," a judgment that has led to the enactment of anti-homosexual laws and policies too often upheld by courts in the name of preserving society's "moral tone."

FOOTNOTES

1. Don Clark in *Men and Masculinity*, Prentice-Hall, p. 88 (1974).
2. *See, e.g., Salt Lake City* v. *Piepenburg*, 571 P. 2d 1299 (Utah 1977), Elliott, Chief Justice:

"Certain justices of the Supreme Court of the United States have said that before a matter can be held to be obscene, it must 'when taken as a whole, lack serious literary, artistic, political or scientific value.' Some state judges, acting the part of sycophants, echo that doctrine. It would appear that such an argument ought only to be advanced by depraved, mentally deficient, mind-warped queers."

3. It is, perhaps, instructive to note that in the McCarthy Era homosexuality was explained as a Communist plot, which justified the witch-hunts of that era. The present regime of the People's Republic of China recently proclaimed that homosexuality is the inevitable product of capitalist decadence.
4. *See, e.g., Marcoli* v. *Schwartz*, 361 N.E. 2d 74 (Ill.1977), a defamation action where the defendant had called plaintiff "a fag," stating that "we don't want any fag working for us." The trial court dismissed the suit on the ground that by "fag" he could have meant "cigarette" or "tire" or "menial".
5. *See, e.g., Inman* v. *City of Miami*, 197 So.2d 50 (Fla.1967), which upheld the constitutionality of an ordinance that prohibits liquor licensees from "knowingly employing a homosexual person" or "knowingly sell to, serve or allow a homosexual person to consume alcoholic beverages, or who knowingly allow two or more homosexual persons to congregate or remain in his place of business." *See also* Oklahoma Statutes, Title 70 (Education Code §6-103.15) which permits the firing of any "teacher, student teacher or teacher's aide" who has "advocated, solicited, imposed, encouraged, or promoted public or private homosexual activity . . . "
6. *See, e.g., Holloway* v. *Arthur Anderson & Co.*, 566 F.2d 659 (9th Cir. 1977) (The Civil Rights Act does not provide a remedy for discrimination based on sexual orientation).
7. *In re Eimers* 358 So. 2d 7 (Fla. 1978) (dissenting opinion).
8. 416 F.Supp. 1350 (Mo.1976) *rev'd* 558 F.2d 848 (8th Cir. 1977); *cert. den.* 98 S.Ct. 1276 (1978).
9. 416 F.Supp. at 1352.
10. *Id.* at 1353.
11. 559 P.2d 1340 (Wash.1977), *cert. denied* 474 U.S. 879 (1977).
12. At the beginning of 1979, twenty-three states had decriminalized private, sexual activity between consenting adults. It is interesting to note that all but one of those states, Illinois, have also ratified the Equal Rights Amendment.
13. 559 P.2d at 1343 (emphasis added).
14. 25 Henry 8, chapter 6. The statute made it a capital felony "to commit the detestable and abominable vice of buggery with mankind or beast." Quoted by Louis Crompton in "Homosexuals and the Death Penalty in Colonial America," *Journal of Homosexuality*, 1976, *1*(3) 277-278.
15. Virginia in 1792 adopted the following:

". . . if any do commit the detestable and abominable vice of Buggery, with man or beast, he or she so offending, shall be adjudged a felon, and shall suffer death, as in the case of felony, without benefit of Clergy." See, *Katz*, Gay American History, *Crowell Press, 1977*.

16. *People* v. *Lindsey.* 310 So. 2d 89 (La. 1975).

17. *People* v. *Rodriguez*, 63 Cal.App. 3d (1976).
18. *People* v. *Lockage*, 109 N.E.2d 39 (Ill.1952).
19. *Dawson* v. *Vance*, 329 F.Supp. 1320 (S.D.Tex. 1971).
20. *Dist. of Columbia* v. *Garcia*, 335 A.2d 217 (D.C.1974).
21. *Silva* v. *Municipal Court*, 40 Cal.App. 3d 733 (1974).
22. *State* v. *Stokes*, 163 S.E.2d 770 (N.C.1968).
23. *Compare, State* v. *Forquer*, 58 N.E.2d 696 (Ohio 1944) (not included) *with Parris* v. *State*, 190 So.2d 564 (Ala.1966) (included).
24. *Compare Prindle* v. *State* 21 S.W. 360 (Tex. 1893) (not included) *with People* v. *Dietz* 343 P.2d 539 (Mont. 1959) (included).
25. *State* v. *Pratt* 116 A.2d 924 (Maine 1955) (not included because "no penetration"). *See* Barnett, *Sexual Freedom and the Constitution*, University of New Mexico Press, pp. 21-25. (1973).
26. *State* v. *Berryman*, 235 P.2d 558 (Okla.1955).
27. W. Barnett, *Sexual Freedom and the Constitution*, University of New Mexico Press, p.23, 1973.
28. *People* v. *Lindsey*, 310 So.2d 89 (La.1975). The court explained that "To meet the test of constitutionality it is not necessary that the statute describe the loathsome and disgusting details connected with each and every way in which unnatural copulation may be accomplished."
29. Many societies have accepted homosexuality as a perfectly natural expression of sexual appetite. *See, e.g.*, Berzon and Leighton *Positively Gay*, Celestial Arts, 1979.
30. *See Report of the Committee on Homosexual Offences and Prostitution*, London 1957.
31. *See, e.g.*, Sullivan, *Attempted Repeals of Gay Rights Ordinances, 4 SexuaLaw Reporter* 61 (1978).
32. *Schlegel* v. *United States*, 416 F.2d 1372, 1373 (Ct.Cl.1969).
33. *Gaylord* v. *Tacoma School Dist.*, 559 P.2d 1340 (Wash.1977) (emphasis added).
34. *Id.* at 1343.
35. 317 F.2d 582 (D.C.Cir.1963).
36. *Id.* at 585.
37. *See, e.g.*, Chaitin and Lefcourt, *Is Gay Suspect?* 8 *Lincoln L. Rev.* 24 (1973).
38. *See., e.g.*, *Anonymous* v. *Macy* 393 F.2d 317 (5th Cir. 1968).
39. *Norton* v. *Macy*, F.2d 1161, 1165 (D.C. Cir. 1969).
40. *See* Siniscalco, *Homosexual Discrimination in Employment*, 16 *Santa Clara L.Rev.* 495 (1976).
41. *Society for Individual Rights, Inc.* v. *Hampton*, 63 F.R.D. 399 (N.D. Cal. 1973).
42. On December 15, 1973, the Trustees of the American Psychiatric Association adopted a resolution stating that "homosexuality per se implies no impairment in judgment, stability, reliability, or general social or vocational capabilities." The Association urged the enactment of civil rights legislation that "would offer homosexual citizens the same protections now guaranteed to others." The American Psychological Association followed in 1975 in a statement which "deplores all public and private discrimination in such areas as employment, housing, public accomodation, and licensing against those who engage in or have engaged in homosexual activities." For an account of the events leading up to these actions, *see* Clark, *Loving Someone Gay*, Celestial Press, 1977.
43. *See, e.g.*, *McKeand* v. *Laird*, 490 F.2d 1262 (9th Cir. 1973); Note, *Security Clearances for Homosexuals*, 25 *Stan. L.Rev.* 403 (1973).
44. 412 F.2d 674 (D.C. Cir.1969).
45. *Id.* at 677.
46. *Crawford* v. *Davis*, 249 F.Supp. 943 (Penn.1966).
47. *Ingalls* v. *Brown*, 377 F.2d 151 (D.C. Cir. 1967).

22

48. 366 A.2d 1337 (N.J.1976); *cert. denied* 434 U.S. 879 (1977).
49. 366 A.2d at 1339.
50. *See* note 11, *supra*.
51. *Boutilier* v. *INS*, 387 U.S. 188, 192 (1967).
52. *See, e.g., In Re Brodie*, 394 F.Supp. 1208 (D.Ore.1975).
53. U.S. Senate Report, 81st Cong., 2nd Session (1950).
54. *Ratchford* v. *Gay Lib*, 98 S.Ct. 1276, 1278 (1978).
55. *Brass* v. *Hoberman*, 295 F.Supp. 358 (S.D.N.Y. 1968).
56. *Richardson* v. *Hampton*, 345 F.Supp. 600 (D.C. 1972).
57. Note, *Is Government Policy Affecting the Employment of Homosexuals Rational?* 48 No. Carolina L.Rev. 912 (1970).
58. *E.g., Inman* v. *City of Miami*, 197 So.2d 50 (Fla. 1967); *Paddock Bar* v. *Div. of ABC*, 134 A.2d 779 (1957).
59. *See, e.g., A.* v. *A.*, 514 P.2d 358 (Ore.1973); *Note, The Avowed Homosexual Mother and Her Right to Child Custody: A Constitutional Challenge That Can No Longer Be Denied*, 12 San Diego L. Rev. 799 (1975).
60. In re Miller____Mich.____(1979).
61. 197 So.2d 50, 53 (Fla.1967) (emphasis added).
62. *The Consenting Adult Homosexual and the Law: An Empirical Study of Enforcement and Administration in Los Angeles County*, 13 U.C.L.A. L.Rev. 644 (1966).
63. Constitutional challenges to the registration and solicitation laws are presently under consideration by the California Supreme Court. *See Pryor* v. *Muni. Ct.*, Sup. Ct. No. LA 30901 and *In Re Anders*, Sup. Ct. Crim. No. 20198.
64. *See* text accompanying notes 39-41 *supra*.
65. Brief for the government in *Saal* v. *Middendorf*, U.S. Ct. of Appeals, 9th Cir., No. 77-2461 (1978).
66. *See* generally *Loving* v. *Virginia*, 388 U.S. 1 (1967).
67. *See, e.g., Boone* v. *Boone* 565 P.2d 337 (N.M. 1977).
68. Kenworthy, *The Case Against Army Segregation*, 275 Annals of the American Academy of Political and Social Science 27 (1951).
69. *See* generally Hunter and Polikoff, *Custody Rights of Lesbian Mothers: Legal Theory and Litigation Strategy* 25 Buffalo L. Rev. 691 (1976).
70. Civ. Action #76-944, U.S. Dist.Ct., D.C. (1977).
71. *Adams* v. *Laird*, 420 F.2d 230 (D.C.Cir.1969).
72. *Weir* v. *U.S.*, 474 F. 2d 617 (Ct. Cl. 1973).
73. Wilkinson and White, *Constitutional Protection for Personal Lifestyles*, 62 Cornell L.Q. 562, 596 (1977).
74. *Doe* v. *Commonwealth's Attorney*, 403 F. Supp. 1259 (E.D. Va. 1975); *affirmed*, 96 S. Ct. 1489 (1976).
75. *Ratchford* v. *Gay Lib*, 98 S. Ct. 1276. 1278 (1978).
76. California Supreme Court, No. S.F. 23625 (1979). (At the time this book went to press, neither decision had been published so citations to page references were impossible.)
77. U.S. Court of Appeals, 9th Cir., Nos. 77-1109, 1204, 1662 (1979). *See* note 76 *supra*.
78. Title VII provides protection against discrimination by employers, employment agencies, and labor organizations on the basis of race, color, religion, sex, or national origin. The Fair Employment Practices Act applies to discrimination by employers, employment agencies, or labor organizations on the basis of race, religious creed, color, national origin, ancestry, or sex.
79. *Holloway* v. *Arthur Anderson & Co.*, 566 F.2d 659, 663 (9th Cir. 1977).
80. *Doe* v. *Commonwealth's Attorney*, 403 F.Supp. 1259 (E.D.Va. 1975) aff'd 96 S.Ct. 1489 (1976).

81. *See, e.g., Singer* v. *U.S. Civil Service Comm'n,* 530 F.2d 247 (9th Cir. 1976) *vacated,* 97 S.Ct. 725 (1977). *See, also, McConnell* v. *Anderson,* 451 F.2d 193 (8th Cir. 1971).

THE LEGAL ARENA:
PROGRESS FOR GAY CIVIL RIGHTS

Dominick Vetri, J.D.

"What do we want?"
"Gay rights!"
"When do we want it?"
"Right now!"

So go the calls and responses in gay pride marches and demonstrations across the country. "Gay rights" has become the rallying cry for demanding an end to all the myriad forms of oppression our society has imposed upon homosexual men and women. The catchphrase "gay rights," however, is actually a misnomer in the legal context, because, contrary to the assertions of some, the gay community does not seek special legal protection but simply equal treatment without regard to one's sexual orientation — heterosexual or homosexual. As applied to law, "gay rights" means an end to all the public and private discrimination previously sanctioned in statutes, regulations, and judicial decisions.

The law as it relates to gay persons involves a number of separate legal issues. The constitutionality of laws that criminalize private, consensual, sexual conduct by adults of the same sex is only one question of concern. Other legal problem areas include: equal opportunity in public and private employment; occupational licensing; family law issues such as marriage, child custody, child visitation rights, adoption, and financial support after separation; housing; public accommodations access; immigration and naturalization; rights of association and free speech; armed services policies; police harassment; income tax status; and insurance coverage. While separate, all of these areas are, of course, interrelated because prejudicial attitudes permeate the legal framework. Furthermore, the continued criminalization of same sex sexual conduct in the majority of states taints all gay people as "criminals" and prevents unbiased evaluation of the other legal issues. Separation of the topics, however, is essential for lawyering purposes in developing a clear analysis of each problem area, in determining the relevant legal provisions and rules, in formulating the most appropriate methods and arguments to challenge discriminatory laws, and in making incremental progress. The American Civil Liberties Union Handbook, *The Rights of*

Mr. Vetri is Professor of Law, University of Oregon, Eugene, Oregon 97403.

Gay People,[1] published in 1975, was the first work to attempt to deal comprehensively with many of these legal issues. In reading the book it is certainly disconcerting to a gay person to learn of the numerous areas in which the law, as of that time, provided no protection against discrimination on the basis of sexual orientation. Some legal progress has been made since the Handbook was published.

The electoral victories for gay people in California and Seattle brightened considerably the outlook for civil rights protection after the bleak days of Miami, St. Paul, Wichita and Eugene. Moreover, the discouraging attitude displayed by the United States Supreme Court in recent gay rights cases may have its brighter side, too.

First, the bad news regarding the Supreme Court cases themselves. A lower court's decision upholding the constitutionality of Virginia's sodomy statute was summarily affirmed in *Doe* v. *Commonwealth's Att'y.*[2] In *Gaylord* v. *Tacoma School Dist.,*[3] a Washington state case dismissing a public school teacher because he was homosexual, the Court denied certiorari. Certiorari was also denied in a New Jersey case ordering a gay schoolteacher to undergo a psychiatric examination because of his leadership of a gay civil rights group, *Gish* v. *Board of Education.*[4] And finally, in *Enslin* v. *Wallford,*[5] certiorari was denied in a case where police in Louisiana had entrapped the defendant into violating the sodomy law with a 17-year-old marine who had consented to the sexual conduct.

The good news is that the Supreme Court's actions in the foregoing cases were essentially procedural and not on the merits. Thus, the Court has not yet spoken definitively on any legal issue of direct importance to the gay community, including the constitutionality of statues that criminalize consensual sexual conduct by adults in private. It can be demonstrated readily that the decisions in *Doe, Gaylord, Gish* and *Enslin,* damaging though they may be, must be viewed as isolated and without permanent impact. The magnitude of the Court's caseload has required it to use procedural devices such as the summary affirmance and certiorari denial to reduce to a manageable number the docket of cases to be decided by full review and written opinions. Annually, out of the approximately 4,000 petitions for review, the Court accepts only about 150 cases to be disposed of by written opinion. Summary affirmances bear little, if any, precedential value as compared to written opinions rendered on the merits after full presentation of written and oral arguments by the parties,[6] and denials of certiorari are accorded no precedential weight at all.[7]

Moreover, beyond using these procedures as a means of docket control, the Court also uses them as a means of selecting the most timely moment to address delicate constitutional issues, such as restrictions on the availability of contraceptives, abortion, capital punishment and, undoubtedly, gay civil rights.[8] Indeed, Justice Brennan, in a 1977 opinion striking down a New York statute regulating the sale and distribution of contraceptives, acknowledged in a propitious footnote that the constitutionality of sodomy laws was still an undecided issue:

[T]he Court has not definitely answered the difficult question whether and to what extent the Constitution prohibits statutes regarding such [private consensual sexual] behavior among adults.[9]

A decision on this question is clearly the single most important legal issue to gay liberation and will likely be the keystone to upsetting all other forms of gay discrimination. We should not be totally disheartened that the Court has not yet decided to hear this important issue of constitutional privacy. Hopefully, an enlightened Supreme Court will decide the issue soon.

In the meantime there have been a number of court decisions, favorable to homosexual men and women, that have not generated nearly as much publicity as the procedural dispositions of the Supreme Court. A welcome and beneficial change that is becoming increasingly clear is that gay people are more and more willing to challenge discrimination by going to court. In the public employment context, there has been a significant number of judicial rulings that termination solely because of the employee's homosexuality is impermissible. *Norton* v. *Macy*[10] was the first decision to hold that the constitutional rule that a public employee's terms of employment be reasonable and non-discriminatory applied to the case of a public employee discharged for immorality on the ground of homosexual conduct. The court ruled that an employee's alleged immoral or indecent conduct can support a dismissal only if it can be shown to have some ascertainable deleterious effect upon the efficiency of the employment. Judge Bazelon propelled gay civil rights forward by his compelling statement:

[T]he notion that it could be an appropriate function of the federal bureaucracy to enforce the majority's conventional codes of conduct in the private lives of its employees is at war with elementary concepts of liberty, privacy and diversity.[11]

Norton was quickly followed by a California ruling, *Morrison* v. *State Board of Education*,[12] that a constitutional right to privacy prohibits sweeping inquiries into a public employee's private life unless the activities in question are substantially related to job performance. *Acanfora* v. *Board of Education of Montgomery County*[13] and *Burton* v. *Cascade School District*,[14] in 1973 and 1975 respectively, also were supportive of the gay public employee's rights. More recently, a Delaware federal district court held that a university teacher's constitutional rights had been infringed by a refusal to renew his contract after he chose to speak out on issues related to gay liberation.[15] The United States Civil Service Commission ruled on July 21, 1978, that homosexuality is not a sufficient ground for dismissal of an employee who is performing his job satisfactorily.[16] A federal judge in December, 1978 held that 6 police officers were improperly fired by the city of Boise, Idaho, merely because they admitted they were lesbian.[17] And on December 6, 1978, the United States Court of Appeals in Washington, D.C., in the case involving Sergeant Matlovich, ruled unanimously that the military service cannot discharge gay persons without specifying appropriate reasons in addition to their homosexuality.[18]

Three U.S. Courts of Appeals have upheld the First Amendment right to university recognition of gay student organizations whose members advocated an end to legal restrictions on homosexual conduct and sought to generate understanding and acceptance of gay people.[19] Another judicial victory occurred when the Florida Supreme Court recently joined New York in ruling that the homosexuality of a candidate is not a sufficient basis for denying admission to the legal profession.[20] A federal district court in Texas held that persons may not be denied the right to become naturalized citizens simply because they are homosexual.[21] Another federal district court concluded that police surveillance and harassment of gay people is a violation of the Federal Civil Rights Act.[22]

There is also progress in the area of family law. A homosexual parent, after divorce, finds it increasingly likely they will be awarded legal custody of the children. A lesbian mother was granted custody of her children in an important decision by the Michigan Supreme Court in January, 1979.[23] Also, a divided Washington Supreme Court has allowed a custody award to a lesbian mother to stand.[24] An openly gay male couple was permitted to adopt a child by the Los Angeles Superior Court.[25] In California, following the landmark *Marvin* decision to award alimony based on a common-law relationship, a trial judge recognized the relation of two gay women as sufficiently legitimate to require one of the women to pay support ("alimony") to the other when the relationship ended.[26]

Recognition should also be given to the *State* v. *Saunders* decision, in which the New Jersey Supreme Court declared unconstitutional the state fornication statute on the ground that it infringed the fundamental right of privacy without any compelling state interest to justify the infringement.[27] This opinion is especially innovative because it identifies the underlying premise of the constitutional right to privacy as being "individual autonomy," and not "personal decisions concerning procreative matters," as other courts had held previously. The use of the "procreative personal decision" rationale in earlier privacy cases involving the availability of contraceptives and abortion can now be seen as merely one manifestation of the grander, more logical principle of "individual autonomy." Justice Pashman put it eloquently:

Private personal acts between two consenting adults are not to be lightly meddled with by the State. The right of personal autonomy is fundamental to a free society. Persons who view fornication as opprobrious conduct may seek strenuously to dissuade people from engaging in it. However, they may not inhibit such conduct through the coercive power of the criminal law. As aptly stated by Sir Francis Bacon, "(t)he sum of behavior is to retain a man's own dignity without intruding on the liberty of others.[28]

Saunders has appropriately been followed by *State* v. *Ciufinni,* a lower court decision in New Jersey, which held that application of the "assault with intent to commit sodomy," statute to a consensual act betwen adults in private is unconstitutional.[29]

There has been improvement in the regulatory and private areas as well. The U.S. Civil Rights Commission has agreed to take jurisdiction over cases of unequal administration of the law based on sexual orientation discrimination, e.g., police harassment of gay men and women, maltreatment of homosexual prisoners, child custody cases involving gay parents, and selective enforcement of sodomy laws.[30] The Internal Revenue Service has revised its regulations to allow tax-exempt status to gay non-profit organizations.[31] The Immigration and Naturalization Service will no longer deny naturalization to homosexual persons on a basis of immorality per se.[32] The Civil Service Commission and the State Department have eliminated their official discriminatory employment policies.[33] Gay people may now leave the military service with honorable discharges.[34] Gay veterans with less than honorable administrative discharges may seek an upgrading of the discharges.[35] New Navy regulations state that it is not mandatory to discharge homosexuals.[36] Of considerable importance, too, is the recent proposal of the FCC to recognize the gay community as an important minority group that must be consulted by TV and radio stations to meet public service requirements.[37]

A large number of universities have adopted policies of non-discrimination on the basis of sexual orientation. The Yale and N.Y.U. law schools voted to deny placement facilities to law firms that discriminate against gay people. Significantly, major corporations including IBM, Exxon, GM, GE, Ford, Texaco, Mobil, Gulf Oil, Dupont, Union Carbide, Dow Chemical, Eastern Airlines, McDonald's, Bell System, Adolph Coors Co., NBC, and Bank of America have quietly adopted policies of non-discrimination. A recent survey of the "Fortune 500" indicated that 122 of America's largest companies have equal opportunity policies regarding homosexual employees.[38]

It also needs to be mentioned that since the vote in Dade County, Florida, there have been far more adoptions of civil rights legislation by municipalities than there have been rejections through referenda. Detroit, the fifth largest city in the U.S., as well as San Francisco and Berkeley recently joined the esteemed rank of enlightened cities. Additionally, New York's Mayor Koch issued an executive order in January, 1978, barring sexual orientation discrimination in city employment. The pressure for gay civil rights is also being maintained in Congress; a bill protecting homosexual men and women against discrimination in employment, housing and public accommodations has again been submitted.[39]

Reversals notwithstanding, it can be said that the degree of legal progress is truly remarkable. Clearly, there have been cross-currents at work in our society. How has this progress been accomplished in so short a time? Considerable credit must be given to gay activism, which has encouraged change through education and lobbying efforts. Judicial attitudes and, consequently, judicial decisions will change as public attitudes change. The guidance and leadership on gay rights must begin not with the courts but with the educational, political and social processes. Grand constitutional decisions, as in the desegregation and abortion cases, typically follow evolving public mores. Such decisions may precede majority support, in fact may help to bring about such support. Nonetheless, judicial decisions follow, rather than lead, changing social values. This underscores why the timeliness of a constitutional issue is of such importance to the Supreme Court.

Credit is also due the writers who have begun to give scholarly attention to the legal rights of homosexual men and women. Only a few years ago, the dearth in the literature of legal analysis of gay rights was a hindrance to progress. The numerous law journal articles and books now being published accomplish several important objectives: (1) In examining the problems in detail, authors help lawyers and judges by describing the precise issues and by developing the relevant considerations for analysis in the decision making process. (2) Scholarly criticism of judicial decisions helps to restrain judges from giving free rein to personal prejudice, for fear that the opinions will be carefully scrutinized. (3) Such publications generate new and creative legal analyses so important to the growth of the law and to the eventual abolition of the many forms of legal oppression of gay people.

One book of legal scholarship should be singled out for recognition because it accomplishes all these objectives and more. That book is Professor Walter Barnett's *Sexual Freedom and the Constitution*.[40] It is a comprehensive and profound examination of the constitutional theories that could be used to challenge laws that presently criminalize consensual homosexual conduct by adults in private. The reader of Barnett's work acquires a sense of how constitutional principles have been evaded by the courts over the years in a systematic sanctioning of the oppression of homosexual people. The law itself has been one of society's invidious tools for discriminating.

Barnett's in-depth analysis shows that sodomy statutes raise many serious constitutional issues: (1) vagueness, (2) the right of privacy, (3) the establishment of religion, (4) equal protection of the laws, and (5) cruel and unusual punishment. In 1973, when Barnett's book was first published, only seven states had legislatively ended the criminalization of consensual sodomy by adults in private; today, that number has increased to twenty-one.[41] Here is significant groundwork for the liberating constitutional ruling that will eventually come from the Supreme Court.

The scholarship of Professor Barnett and other more recent legal writers demonstrates that, in Barnett's words, "persuasive arguments can be made for the constitutional invalidation of that bulwark of anti-homosexual legislation — the sodomy laws — on which rests much of the edifice of other discrimination"[42] against homosexual men and women. We await the day in the near future when these arguments are implemented by a decision of the United States Supreme Court. But we shall continue to make substantial legal progress, as illustrated, pending that eventful day.

FOOTNOTES

1. American Civil Liberties Union Handbook, *The Rights of Gay People*. Avon Books, 1975 (paperback). The authors are E. Carrington Boggan, Marilyn G. Haft, Charles Lister, and John P. Rupp.
2. *Doe v. Commonwealth Att'y for Richmond*, 403 F. Supp. 1199 (E.D. Va. 1975), summarily aff'd without opinion, 425 U.S. 901 (1976).
3. *Gaylord v. Tacoma Dist. No. 10*, 559 P.2d 1340 (Wash. 1977), cert. denied, 98 S. Ct. 234 (1978).
4. *Gish v. Bd. of Educ. of the Borough of Paramus*, Bergen County, 366 A.2d 1337 (N.J. App. Div. 1976), cert. denied, 98 S. Ct. 233 (1978).
5. *Enslin v. Wallford*, 565 F.2d 156 (4th Cir. 1977), cert. denied, 98 S. Ct. 2252 (1978).
6. *Fusari v. Steinberg*, 419 U.S. 379, 390, 391-92 (1974) (concurring opinion of Chief Justice Burger): "Indeed upon fuller consideration of an issue under plenary review, the Court has not hesitated to discard a rule which a line of summary affirmances may appear to have established." *Edelman v. Jordan*, 415 U.S. 651, 671 (1974) (Justice Rehnquist): summary affirmances "obviously . . . are not of the same precedential value as would be an opinion of this Court treating the question on the merits."
7. See *Brown v. Allen*, 344 U.S. 443, 489-97 (opinion of Justice Frankfurter) and at 542-43 (opinion of Justice Jackson) (1953); see also *Maryland v. Baltimore Radio Show, Inc.*, 338 U.S. 912 (1950) (opinion of Justice Frankfurter).
8. It should not be overlooked that the Court by denying certiorari in a 1977 case let stand a Court of Appeals decision upholding the constitutional right of a gay student organization to official recognition at a state university. *Gay Lib v. Univ. of Missouri*, 416 F. Supp. 1350 (W.D. Mo. 1976), rev'd, 558 F2d 848 (8th Cir. 1977), cert. denied sub. nom, 98 S. Ct. 1276 (1978).
9. *Carey v. Population Services Int'l*, 431 U.S. 678, 694, n. 17 (1977).

10. *Norton* v. *Macy*, 417 F2d 1161 (D.C. Cir. 1969).
11. *Id.* at 1166.
12. *Morrison* v. *State Board of Education*, 1 Cal.3d 214, 461 P.2d 375 (1969).
13. *Acanfora* v. *Board of Education of Montgomery County*, 359 F. Supp. 843 (D. Md. 1973).
14. *Burton* v. *Cascade School Dist. Union High School No. 5*, 512 F.2d 850 (9th Cir.), cert. denied, 423 U.S. 839 (1975).
15. *Aumiller* v. *University of Delaware*, 434 F. Supp. 1273 (D. Del. 1977).
16. The ruling overturned the prior decision, which had removed clerk-typist John E. Singer from his job with the Equal Employment Opportunity Commission. 4 *Sexual Law Reporter* 50 (1978). For the earlier litigation see *Singer* v. *U.S. Civil Service Comm'n*, 530 F.2d 247 (9th Cir. 1976), judgment vacated for reconsideration in light of regulation changes, 429 U.S. 1034 (1977). See also note 33 *infra*.
17. *The Advocate*, No. 258 at 16 (Jan. 11, 1979).
18. *Matlovich* v. *Secretary of the Air Force*, 47 U.S. Law Week 2631 (D.C. Ct. App., Dec. 6, 1978).
19. *Gay Lib* v. *Univ. of Missouri*, 416 F. Supp. 1350 (W.D. Mo. 1976), rev'd, 558, F. 2d 848 (8th Cir. 1977), cert. denied dub. nom., 98 S. Ct. 1276 (1978); *Gay Alliance of Students* v. *Matthews*, 544 F. 2d 162 (4th Cir. 1976); *Gay Students Organization of Univ. of New Hampshire* v. *Bonner*, 509 F2d 652 (1st Cir. 1974).
20. *In re Eimers*, 358 So. 2d 7 (Fla. 1978).
21. *Longstaff* v. *Immigration & Naturalization Service* (N.D. Tex. 1977), *The Advoate*, No. 245 at 12 (July 12, 1978).
22. *Cyr* v. *Walls*, 439 F. Supp. 697 (N.D. Tex. 1977).
23. *Miller* v. *Miller*, 5 Family Law Reporter 2302 (Mich. Sup. Ct., Jan. 17, 1979). The Michigan Supreme Court reversed a lower court order directing that custody of a 12-year old daughter be changed from her mother, a lesbian, to her father. The Court said "the record does not present clear and convincing evidence that the change of custody is in the best interests of the child."
24. *The Advocate*, No. 255 at 8 (Nov. 29, 1978).
25. *The Advocate*, No. 262 at 12 (Mar. 8, 1979).
26. *Richardson* v. *Conley*, California Superior Court (San Diego, June 6, 1978). The two women had participated in a Holy Union ceremony at the Metropolitan Community Church and, earlier, had signed an agreement that one would take responsibility for the household and the other for financial support.
27. *State* v. *Saunders*, 381 A.2d 333 (N.J. 1977).
28. *Id.* at 342. It is, of course, eminently appropriate that the philosophy and language of Sir Francis Bacon should be used in this path-breaking opinion that is to be an important case in ending the legal oppression of gay people. A. L. Rowse, *Homosexuals in History*, 41-49, 65-69 (Macmillan Pub. Co., 1977).
29. *State* v. *Ciuffini*, 395 A.2d 904 (N.J. App. Div. 1978).
30. U.S. Commission on Civil Rights, August 15, 1977 as reported in 4 *Its Time*, No. 1 at 1 (Oct. 1977) (National Gay Task Force Newsletter).
31. Exemptions have been granted to the following organizations, among others: Fund for Human Dignity, 4 *It's Time*, No. 1 at 1 (Oct. 1977) (National Gay Task Force Newsletter); Houston Human Rights Defense Foundation, *The Advocate*, No. 244 at 21 (June 28, 1978); The Human Rights Foundation, *The Advocate*, No. 247 at 10 (Aug. 9, 1978); Gay Rights Advocates, *The Advocate*, No. 248 at 8 (Aug. 23, 1978); Gay Horizons, *The Advocate*, No. 249 at 10 (Sept. 6, 1978).
32. After meetings in 1978 between representatives of the National Gay Task Force, the Immigration and Naturalization Service, and the Surgeon General of the U.S., the U.S. Public Health Service has stopped defining gay people as "sex deviants" or "psychopathic personalities." Health Service border officers, immigration officials,

and State Department visa officers have been advised of the policy change. *The Advocate*, No. 245 at 12 (July 12, 1978). The Immigration and Naturalization Service has changed its naturalization policy so that it no longer recommends to the courts that gay aliens be denied citizenship and the Service has agreed to review its immigration policy. 4 *It's Time*, No. 3 at 1 (Dec. 1977) (National Gay Task Force Newsletter).

33. The Civil Service Commission has removed the word "immoral" from the regulations providing grounds for dismissal. 5 C.F.R. § 731.201(b) (1975) and § 731.202 (1976). The Civil Service also amended *The Suitability Guidelines for Federal Employment* to conform to the regulation to "require that persons not be disqualified from federal employment solely on the basis of homosexual conduct." The Guidelines now provide:

Court decisions require that persons not be disqualified from Federal employment solely on the basis of homosexual conduct. The Commission and agencies have been enjoined not to find a person unsuitable for Federal employment solely because that person is homosexual or has engaged in homosexual acts. Based upon these court decisions and outstanding injunction, while a person may not be found unsuitable based on unsubstantial conclusions concerning possible embarrassment to the Federal service, a person may be dismissed or found unsuitable for Federal employment where the evidence establishes that such person's sexual conduct affects job fitness. Recently (July 21, 1978) the Civil Service Commission ordered Singer, a federal employee, reinstated based on the new Guidelines, See: *The Advocate*, No. 249 at 8 (Sept., 6, 1978). Singer had been dismissed under the pre-existing regulations on the grounds that he had been openly gay. He initially lost before the Commission and subsequently lost in his federal district court action; the trial court's decision was affirmed by the Court of Appeals, but the Supreme Court remanded for reconsideration in light of the new regulation and guidelines that had become effective in the interim. *Singer* v. *U.S. Civil Service Comm'n*, 530 F. 2d 247 (9th Cir. 1976), remanded for reconsideration, 429 U.S. 1034 (1977). The U.S. Agency for International Development, an agency of the State Department, has abolished its policy of excluding gay people from employment. The new policy declares that "homosexuals as a class are not unsuitable for employment" and that "private homosexual conduct will not be grounds for dismissal from employment when an employee has a sound record." Importantly, it was stated that an openly gay person cannot be found to be a security risk. *The Advocate*, No. 227 at 10 (Nov. 2, 1977).

34. *The Adovcate*, No. 251 at 8 (Oct. 4, 1978).
35. *Ibid.*
36. 4 *Sexual Law Reporter* 60 at n. 11 (1978). The regulations do provide, however, that discharge will be the ordinary action. But *Matlovich* v. *Secretary of the Air Force supra* n. 18 will now have to be reckoned with.
37. 43 C.F.R. 35, 357 (1978) (to be codified in 47 C.F.R. §73).
38. 5 *It's Time*, No. 9 at 1 (Nov. 1978) (National Gay Task Force Newsletter).
39. House Bill 2074, 96th Congress (1979). The bill this session has 40 co-sponsors.
40. Walter Barnett, *Sexual Freedom and the Constitution*. Univ. of New Mexico Press, 1973.
41. Alaska, California, Colorado, Connecticut, Delaware, Hawaii, Illinois, Indiana, Iowa, Maine, Nebraska, New Hampshire, New Jersey, New Mexico, North Dakota, Ohio, Oregon, South Dakota, Washington, and West Virginia. Alaska's repeal is effective January 1, 1980. Missouri has reduced consensual sodomy by adults in private from a felony to misdemeanor status. See generally Note, "The Constitutionality of Sodomy Statutes," 45 Fordham L. Rev. 553, 570 at n. 93 (1976).
42. *Supra* note 40 at 313.

ADDENDUM

***The landmark decision by the California Supreme Court in *Gay Law Students Ass'n* v. *Pacific Telephone & Telegraph,* 156 Cal. Rptr. 14 (Calif., May 31, 1979), was handed down too late for inclusion in the text of the article. The case is a major breakthrough in the area of employment discrimination. This important case held that the California equal protection clause does not permit privately owned utilities (or the state) to arbitrarily discriminate against homosexuals regarding employment. This is the first time that the equal protection clause has been used by a state supreme court in protecting gay men and women as a class. Additionally the decision went further in concluding that employment discrimination against an individual who openly acknowledges his or her homosexuality and works for gay civil rights is in violation of California's Labor Code provision prohibiting discrimination by *public and private* employers based on an employee's political activities.

PERCEPTIONS OF HOMOSEXUALITY
BY JUSTICES OF THE PEACE IN
COLONIAL VIRGINIA

Robert Oaks, Ph.D.

Laws forbidding homosexuality to varying degrees exist in all states today, and in most of these states even private homosexual activity between consenting adults is illegal. The laws have a long tradition that reflects the customs and attitudes of society as a whole. Many of the justifications for these laws, especially medical and theological, have been eroded considerably in recent years, forcing the proponents of the laws to fall back upon custom, tradition, social or moral "norms," and history. When we study history carefully, however, it becomes clear that many of our traditions in the area of sexuality derive from ideas that are three or four hundred years old and that appear ludicrous in light of contemporary knowledge.

It is extremely difficult for the historian to find sources for determining attitudes and beliefs about the nature of homosexuality before the twentieth century. People wrote as little as possible about the "wickedness not to be named." One way to discover attitudes, as Louis Crompton has shown, is to study the laws themselves. Crompton's survey of Colonial America, where, in accordance with English precedent or biblical injunctions, homosexuality was a capital offense, reveals a deep-seated animosity. In Puritan New England, legislators usually incorporated verbatim into statutes the proscriptions of Leviticus. In the Southern colonies, English laws either were confirmed by colonial legislatures or assumed to be incorporated in the common law. In every colony, except for a brief period in early eighteenth-century Pennsylvania, "the crime against nature" was a capital offense. While it is true that this penalty was seldom enforced, the fact that it remained on the books until long after the American Revolution indicates the intensity of the horror surrounding this "crime." [1]

Despite their historical value as illustrations of attitudes, laws generally reveal little concerning people's deeper beliefs about homosexuality.

Dr. Oaks received his M.A. from U.C.L.A. and his Ph.D. from the University of Southern California in 1970.

Obviously it was thought to be "detestable," a sin, a horrible crime, but the laws themselves rarely theorize about the causes or the nature of this crime. A more revealing picture emerges from handbooks published to explain laws to justices of the peace, men who seldom had had any formal legal training. As the principal enforcers of law at the local level, justices of the peace inherited a long history carried over into most of the American colonies from England. Because these officials usually came from the most influential families, their interpretations of the handbooks were widely credited.

The institution of justice of the peace was especially strong in Virginia, which by the eighteenth century was the largest and in many ways the most "English" of the colonies. Unlike other colonies, particularly the northern ones, Virginia did not have a law dealing specifically with sexual offenses. Instead, the colony relied on the English "buggery" statute of 1533.[2] Usually referred to as "25 Henry 8, chapter 6," this statute made the "detestable and abominable Vice of Buggery" (defined as sodomy between two men or as bestiality by men or women) a capital offense. The law stemmed from Henry VIII's attack on the church and made homosexuality, previously punishable only in ecclesiastical courts as a sin against God, punishable now in civil courts as a crime against the English state. Henry had taken the first step toward weakening the church by depriving it of its judicial powers.[3] When one considers the attitude of most churches in twentieth-century America, there is considerable irony in the fact that homosexuality became a civil crime in England in order to strengthen the state and to weaken the power and influence of the church.

Shortly after the passage of the law, handbooks for justices of the peace in England incorporated the new crime:

It is enacted that the vice of Buggorie committed with mankynde, or beast be adjudged felonie, and that no person so offendying that be admytted to his clergye. And that the Justices of peace that have power to here and determine the same, as other felonies.[4]

The refusal to allow "benefit of clergy" specifically denied convicted "buggerers" the opportunity, available in connection with many other capital offenses, to escape the death penalty for their first conviction. Several handbooks published later in the sixteenth century contained similar language, but none described the origin or nature of the crime.[5]

In 1628 the great English jurist Sir Edward Coke, expounding in his *Institutes* on all English laws, gave semi-official sanction to contemporary attitudes and beliefs about homosexuality and influenced justices of the peace on both sides of the Atlantic for the next two hundred years. In the Third Part of the *Institutes*, Coke reinvoked religious abhorrence of the crime by stating that it was "against the ordinance of the Creator and order of nature." He was among the first to attribute buggery to the Italians, who presumably had caught it or had learned to enjoy it from the "Lumbards," and incorrectly traced the derivation of the word "buggery" from the Italian word "bugeria." Coke clarified the method of execution (hanging, as opposed to burning or burying alive) and specified that some evidence of penetration was necessary for conviction. Under English law, therefore, buggery clearly meant anal intercourse between two men. Finally, Coke wrote that if the party buggered were "within the age of discretion" (presumably meaning under fourteen years of age), the boy would not be held guilty of a crime. Englishmen who practiced buggery came to the "abomination," according to Coke, in one of four ways: "by pride, excess of diet, idleness, and contempt of the poor."[6] Proud, fat, lazy, rich men must have been very suspect in seventeenth-century England.

One hundred and fifty years later, handbooks written specifically for Virginia justices of the peace continued to lean heavily on Coke's *Institutes*. Richard Starke's *The Office and Authority of a Justice of Peace*, published in Williamsburg in 1774, devotes one whole section to "buggery." Because Starke's book reveals so much more than do the laws themselves about attitudes on the eve of the Revolution, it is worth quoting at some length:

THIS Word is derived from the Italian Bugarone, *the Vice being said to have been first introduced into* England *by the* Lombards *from* Italy.

Buggery is a detestable and abominable Sin, Among Christians not to be named, committed by carnal Knowledge, against the Ordinance of the Creator, and Order of Nature, by Mankind with Mankind, or with Brute Beast, or with Womankind with Brute Beast. 3. Inst. 58.

By the Statute of 25, Hen. VIII. Chap. 6, Buggery committed with Mankind, or Beast, is made Felony without Benefit of Clergy; and this Statute making it Felony generally, there may be Accessories both before and after. But those who are present, aiding, and abetting, are all Principals; and although none of the Principals are admitted to their Clergy, yet Accessories before and after are not excluded from Clergy. 1. H.H. 670.

If the Party buggered be within the Age of Discretion (which is generally reckoned the Age of fourteen) it is no Felony in him, but in the Agent only; but if Buggery be committed upon a Man of the Age of Discretion, it is Felony in them both. 3 Inst. 59. 1 H.H. 670.

The Heinousness of this Crime (Happily indeed but little known heretofore in this Colony) renders a strict Examination into the Fact, as well as great Caution in bailing the offender, necessary to be observed by the Justices before whom the Information is made . . . .[7]

As had Coke, Starke obviously accepted the long English tradition of associating homosexuality with Italy. Both the English and the Virginians believed homosexuality to be rare at home but widespread in Italy. English parents were warned not to let their sons travel to that country and, when homosexuality seemed to be on the increase in eighteenth-century England, one writer blamed it on the drinking of tea and "the pernicious influence of Italian opera."[8] The association with Italy probably explains why Coke, Starke, and the authors of other American handbooks mistakenly traced the derivation of "buggery" from apparently nonexistent Italian words rather than from a corruption of the term "Bulgar."[9]

In 1792 Virginia, wishing no longer to rely on English laws after the Revolution, passed its own buggery statute: ". . . if any do commit the detestable and abominable vice of Buggery, with man or beast, he or she so offending, shall be adjudged a felon, and shall suffer death, as in case of felony, without benefit of Clergy."[10] When William Walter Hening published a new guidebook for justices of the peace in 1795, his "buggery" section also attributed the origin of both the name and the practice to Italy. Largely ignorant of biology, seventeenth- and eighteenth-century Englishmen and Americans feared bestiality even more than homosexuality because they believed that inhuman creatures could be produced.[11] In specific reference to bestiality, Hening cited an example from Coke, "of a great lady in England, who cohabited with a *Baboon,* and conceived by it."

While repeating the belief that the crime was seldom committed in Virginia, Hening nevertheless provided justices with the form to be used for indictments for buggery:

county to wit.
The jurors for the commonwealth upon their oath do present that _____ *of the county of* _____ *aforesaid, labourer, not having the fear of God before his eyes, nor regarding the order of nature, but being moved and seduced by the instigation of the devil, on the* ____ *day of* ____ *in the year of our Lord* ____ *with force and arms, at the county aforesaid, in and upon one* _____, *a youth about the age of* ____ *years, then and there being, feloniously did make an assault, and then and there feloniously, wickedly, diabolically, and against the order of nature had a venereal affair with the said* _____ *and then and there carnally knew the said* _____ *and then and there feloniously wickedly, and diabolically, and against the order of nature, with the said* _____ *did commit that detestable and abominable crime of buggery (not to be named amongst* Christians) *to the great displeasure of Almighty God, to the great scandal of all human kind, against the form of the statute in such case made and provided, and against the peace and dignity of the commonwealth.*[12]

The indictment was, in some ways, a throwback to an earlier day. For the moment, the Italians were absolved and homosexuality was blamed on the "instigation of the devil." This religious view is all the more striking in light of the section on "Blasphemy and Profaneness," immediately preceding the "Buggery" section. Here Hening referred to the "real pleasure to every friend to civil and religious liberty" resulting from Virginia's abolition of the "crime of *blasphemy* . . . which has disgraced the code of almost every civilized nation in Europe, and was implicitly adopted in America, prior to the late revolution." But now, Hening reported, Thomas Jefferson's work in establishing religious freedom and in separating church from state in Virginia, had done away with this archaic crime.[13] It is also interesting that the indictment form applied only to an adult who committed buggery on a presumably innocent youth. In a later edition Hening mentions animals in a footnote. The implication, of course, is that Hening never imagined that buggery could take place between consenting adults. It would only occur when an adult forced himself upon a boy or an animal. Hening's equation of homosexuality with pederasty, a confusion by no means uncommon in twentieth-century America, went even beyond Coke, who had stipulated that "Amator puerorum . . . is but a species of Buggery."[14]

The Virginia lawmakers, by the way, rejected Jefferson's suggestion of 1776 that the death penalty for sodomy be abolished. His proposal had lumped sodomy with rape and polygamy and called for the "liberalized" penalty of castration for men and cutting a half inch hole in the nasal cartilage of women.[15]

A few years later, in 1800, the Virginia General Assembly revised its penal code and finally repealed the death penalty for buggery, though only for free men. The crime now carried penalties of from one to ten years in prison. Hening incorporated this change in his 1810 edition, although once again he blamed the Italians and repeated the story about the woman and the baboon. Drawing upon Coke's *Institutes*, Hening instructed justices that penetration had to take place before the crime could be considered buggery; emmission of semen, without penetration, did not qualify. Presumably the requirement for penetration had always been in effect in colonial Virginia, but now it was specifically spelled out.[16] "For the honour of human nature," Hening wrote with obvious relief, "it must be observed, that this crime is seldom committed." The requirement for penetration and the obvious difficulty in obtaining proof of it, undoubtedly made indictment unlikely.

The removal of the death penalty did not necessarily reflect a decline in opposition to the crime of buggery. In two hundred years of Virginia's history, there had been only one recorded execution for buggery, and even then (in 1625) there was some doubt as to the guilt of the condemned.[17] Despite the nearly complete absence of prosecutions, Virginia authorities still felt it necessary to keep the crime on the books. Even the new reduced sentence was rather harsh when compared to the penalties for other sexual offenses. Bigamy, for instance, was punishable in the new code by a prison term of six months to two years. Adultery resulted in a twenty dollar fine, fornication in a ten dollar fine. Only rape drew heavier penalties, requiring imprisonment from ten to twenty years when the victim was an adult woman. It is ironical that, according to Hening, rape of a girl under ten, since it was not specifically mentioned in the new statutes, came under the general provision of felonies formerly capital. Thus, rape of a child received the same penalty as buggery, one to ten years, considerably less than rape of an adult. Slaves were singled out for harsher punishment. Attempted rape of a white woman carried a penalty of castration; if the attempt succeeded, the penalty was death.[18]

The handbooks for justices of the peace, even more than the laws themselves, reveal much about attitudes toward homosexuality in colonial Virginia. What remains a mystery, however, especially in light of the paucity of prosecutions, is why the people had so great a fear as to criminalize homosexuality in the first place. Since many of today's assumptions, attitudes, and laws are derived from similarly irrational and ignorant beliefs of the past, we need to continue to look at our history for ways to break down the ignorance and prejudice existing in the present.

FOOTNOTES

I wish to thank Professor Louis Crompton for his suggestions in the preparation of this article.

1. Louis Crompton, "Homosexuals and the Death Penalty in Colonial America," *Journal of Homosexuality*, 1976, *1*(3), 277-293. See also Oaks, "Things Fearful to Name: Sodomy and Buggery in Seventeenth-Century New England," *Journal of Social History*, Winter 1978, pp. 268-281.
2. Arthur P. Scott, *Criminal Law in Colonial Virginia* (Chicago, 1930), p. 284.
3. H. Montgomery Hyde, *The Other Love: An Historical and Contemporary Survey of Homosexuality in Britain* (London, 1970), frontispiece, p. 39; G. Rattray Taylor, *Sex in History* (New York, 1954, 1970), pp. 145-146.
4. Anthony Fitzherbert, *The Newe Boke of Justices of the Peas* (London, 1538; reprint edition New York, 1969), fol. 158.
5. See, for example, . . . *the boke for a Justice of peace* . . . (London, 1544); *The New Book of Iustices of Peace Made by Anthonie Fitzerbert* (London, 1554); *The Auctoritie of al Iustices of Peace* . . . (London, 1580). I consulted the copies in the rare book collection of the Huntington Library, San Marino, California.
6. Hyde, *op. cit.*, p. 37; Sir Edward Coke, *The Third Part of the Institutes of the Laws of England*, 4th ed. (London, 1669), chapter x, pp. 58-59.
7. Richard Starke, *The Office and Authority of a Justice of Peace* (Williamsburg, 1774), p. 61 (Evans #13637).

8. Lawrence Stone, *The Family, Sex and Marriage in England 1500-1800* (New York, 1977), p. 492; *Plain Reasons for the Growth of Sodomy in England,* quoted in Ralph Blair, *Etiological and Treatment Literature on Homosexuality* (New York, 1972), p. 1.

9. Vern L. Bullough, *Sexual Variance in Society and History* (New York, 1976), p. 390.

10. *A Collection of All Such Acts of the General Assembly of Virginia . . . Now in Force* (Richmond, 1803), p. 179.

11. William Waller Hening, *The New Virginia Justice . . .* (Richmond, 1795), p. 93. On fears of bestiality, see Oaks, *op. cit.*

12. Hening, *The New Virginia Justice,* pp. 93-94.

13. *Ibid.,* p. 93.

14. Coke, *op. cit.*

15. Julian P. Boyd, ed., *The Paper of Thomas Jefferson* (Princeton, 1950-), II, 325.

16. William Waller Hening, *The New Virginia Justice . . . ,* 2nd ed. (Richmond, 1810), pp. 147-148.

17. See Crompton, *op. cit.,* pp. 290-292.

18. Hening, *The New Virginia Justice,* 2nd ed., pp. 144-148, 276, 470-475.

HOMOSEXUAL ACTS AND THE
CONSTITUTIONAL RIGHT TO PRIVACY

David A. J. Richards, J.D., D.Phil.

In *Doe* v. *Commonwealth's Attorney for City of Richmond*,[1] the Supreme Court of the United States summarily affirmed the decision by a three-judge court that Virginia's "crimes against nature" statute could constitutionally be applied to private, consensual, homosexual relations between adult males. While the precedential force of the summary affirmance is unclear, some courts have read the Court's action to mean that "unnatural" sex acts are not protected by the evolving constitutional right to privacy. This decision is, I believe, an unprincipled departure from the developing line of case law, which uses the idea of a constitutional right to privacy, and a scandalous lapse from the underlying ethic on which the case law rests. *Doe* is both constitutionally and morally wrong.[2]

One cannot understand the isolation of consensual homosexual acts from constitutional values without first appreciating the force of the idea of "the unnatural." I begin this article, therefore, with an explanation of how the idea has traditionally been misapplied to homosexual acts. Next I examine the moral values underlying the constitutional right to privacy. Finally, I argue that consensual homosexual acts are indeed protected by the ethic of the constitutional right to privacy and that statutes of the kind upheld in *Doe* are constitutionally invalid.

I. THE CONCEPT OF THE UNNATURAL

If we are to debate whether the traditional application of a concept of the unnatural to consensual homosexuals acts can any longer be sustained, we must first understand what people have historically meant by denominating acts "unnatural."

Mr. Richards is Professor of Law at New York University School of Law, New York, New York 10003. He is a graduate of Harvard College and Harvard Law School, and has a D. Phil. from Oxford University. His books include A Theory of Reasons for Action *and* The Moral Criticism of Law.

1. An Explication of the Term "Unnatural"

The term "unnatural" is incomplete, depending for its sense on the *kind* of things to which it is applied (for example, persons, acts, events) and on theoretical notions of proper functioning by that thing. The unnatural, as a concept, implies that the operation of a thing, as explained by a theory of proper process for that thing, has gone awry — has been impaired, frustrated, or corrupted — so radically that we have difficulty understanding how the thing can operate.

The word "unnatural," as applied to human acts, is not the same idea as the irregular or statistically abnormal. If an unnatural act like matricide were practiced with regularity, we might nonetheless regard it as unnatural so long as we considered it a deviation from proper human functioning. Certain experiences — personal affection and commitment, for example — are defined by our theory of what is properly human as being unique to mankind and as central to full human self-realization. Human beings act unnaturally when they gratuitously and willfully deprive themselves or others of such experiences — as when a father knowingly deprives his child of all signs and expressions of affection. Such an action stretches our personal theories of human nature to the breaking point and appears humanly inexplicable.

To the extent that various theories of human nature may identify different human capacities, propensities, and ends as central, differing conceptions of the unnatural result. Shakespeare, for example, believed that rule by an anointed hereditary monarch was a primary human good without which society could not achieve the minimal conditions of order.[3] Consequently, Shakespeare regarded usurpation of an hereditary monarch's power and, of course, regicide as unnatural,[4] for these acts frustrate human purposes as Shakespeare understood them, and terminate the conditions that make life in society possible. Other theories of human nature, not identifying monarchy as a primary human good, would not regard usurpation as unnatural, however immoral or otherwise undesirable.

Typically, theories of human nature do not consider immoral acts as necessarily unnatural, for many forms of immorality are all too characteristically human. Murderers, for example, often act on quite understandable human motives of jealousy, anger, venality, and the like. Such murders are morally wrong, but not unnatural. Although the results achieved do not justify morally the means chosen, we can understand how humans come to make such trade-offs. Only those murders are judged unnatural that achieve ends insignificant when compared to the human goods sacrificed. Thus, intrafamilial murders are commonly regarded as unnatural on the ground that such murders inexplicably sacrifice the primary human good of warm family attachments for relatively paltry reasons. Theft, similarly, is morally wrong, but is considered unnatural only in a case such as a robbery committed by a millionaire "just for kicks." Traditionally, the performance of apparently unnatural acts was thought by simple people of good will to distinguish the human from the inhuman and therefore to degrade the perpetrator to an animal or demon, or to elevate to deity. Using the same logic, if one supposed that the only proper purpose of human sexuality is procreation, it would follow that while fornication may be immoral it is not unnatural, since the procreative purpose is not violated. On the other hand, bestiality and homosexuality are both immoral and unnatural,[5] for they impair, frustrate, or corrupt the procreative process.

2. The Unnatural and Sexual Deviance

The earliest literate argument for calling sexual deviance "unnatural" appears in Plato's *Laws*.[6] Plato contended that homosexual acts between males are unnatural on two grounds: First, such acts undermine the development of desirable masculine character traits—e.g., courage and self-control. This idea probably rested on an assumption that homosexual acts reduce men to the status of women. Second, Plato argued that male sexuality has but one proper use, namely, procreation within marriage, and that homosexuality is unnatural because it is sterile. This latter thought rests on the Greek concept that everything in the physical world has an essential definable function. (For example, Aristotle argued that usury is unnatural because it violates the proper function of money.)[7]

The Christian interpretation of the unnaturalness of homosexuality was consolidated and given a theoretical basis by St. Thomas Aquinas's reformulation of St. Augustine's view that the only proper "genital commotion"[8] is that aimed toward the reproduction of the species in marriage.[9] (Since sexual drives operate quite independently of the will, let alone the will to reproduce, sexuality was a source of continuing shame for St. Augustine.)[10] Building on these Augustinian foundations, St. Thomas argued that, even granting that homosexual acts between consenting adults harm no one, the acts are still unnatural and immoral for they are an offense to God, who has ordained procreation as the only legitimate use of sexuality.[11] St. Thomas takes the Platonic view that human sexuality has a distinct purpose and gives it a theological interpretation: Homosexuality is unnatural not primarily because it degrades proper human function, but because it violates the divine law that sanctions that function.

This Platonic and theological tradition was absorbed into American law through Blackstone, who refused even to mention sexual deviance, referring to it as "the infamous *crime against nature*, committed either with man or beast . . . the very mention of which is a disgrace to human nature."[12] The Blackstonian language of condemnation was imitated in American colonial statutes and continues to be used in statutes of some American states. Whatever the form of the law, the laws of twenty-nine states and the District of Columbia impose criminal penalties on consenting adults who engage in private homosexual activity.

II. THE MORAL VALUES UNDERLYING THE CONSTITUTIONAL RIGHT TO PRIVACY

The idea of an independent constitutional right to privacy was introduced in 1965 in *Griswold* v. *Connecticut*[13] and has been developed in a number of major cases since that time. In *Griswold,* the Supreme Court invalidated a Connecticut statute forbidding the use of contraceptives, as applied to married couples, on the ground that the statute violated a constitutional right to privacy protecting the marital relationship. In 1969 in *Stanely* v. *Georgia,*[14] the Court held unconstitutional a state statute punishing the private possession of obscene materials, citing one's "right to be free, except in very limited circumstances, from unwanted governmental intrusion into one's privacy."[15] In 1972 the Court in *Eisenstadt* v. *Baird*[16] invalidated the conviction of a campus lecturer for giving a contraceptive device to a young woman of undisclosed marital status. The Court noted:

It is true that in Griswold the right to privacy in question inhered in the marital relationship. Yet the married couple is not an independent entity with a mind and heart of its own, but an association of two individuals each with a separate intellectual and emotional makeup. If the right of privacy means anything, it is the right of the individual, *married or single, to be free from unwarranted governmental intrusion into matters so fundamentally affecting a person as the decision whether to bear or beget a child.*[17]

The scope of the right to privacy was further expanded in 1973 in *Roe* v. *Wade,*[18] in which the Court held that a Texas statute forbidding abortion, except to save the life of the mother, violated the mother's fundamental right to privacy.

The constitutional right to privacy clearly turns on some form of substantive liberty to act in certain ways without threat of governmental sanction, interference, or penalty. The Court's remarks about the nature of this substantive right are suggestive. Activities protected by the right include by implication individuals' "beliefs, their thoughts, their emotions and their sensations," central values of the "right to be left alone."[19] These elements are at the core of "protected intimate relationship(s)"[20] and require some kind of sanctury in order to be properly cultivated and perfected.

As contractarian moral theory has, I believe, an authoritative role in the analysis of constitutional values,[21] I turn to such a theory to elucidate the moral and constitutional values underlying the right-to-privacy cases.

For the purpose of this article, moral principles are those that perfectly rational people, irrespective of historical or personal age, in a hypothetical "original position" of equal liberty and having all knowledge and reasonable belief except that of their specific personal situation, would agree are the ultimate standards of conduct applicable at large. Since we intend to apply this definition of moral principles to the development of a theory of justice, we must introduce into the original position the existence of conflicting claims upon a limited supply of goods and consider a specific set of principles to regulate these claims.

"General goods" are those things or conditions that are typically chosen by rational people as the generalized means to a variety of particular desires. Liberty is usually classified as one of these general goods. Similarly, we identify capacities, opportunities, and wealth as general goods.

People desire general goods — liberties, opportunities, wealth — in order to attain self-respect through the fulfillment of their life plan. Self-respect may thus be identified as the primary human good. People in the original position would regulate access to the general goods so as to maximize the likelihood that each member of society will attain self-respect.

The liberties distributed by the principles of justice typically include freedoms of thought and expression (freedoms of speech, the press, religion, and association), civic rights (impartial administration of civil and criminal law in defense of property and person), political rights (the right to vote and participate in political affairs), and freedom of physical, economic, and social movement. The importance of these liberties rests on their relation to the primary good of self-respect, since these liberties nurture personal competence through full expression of the spirit, self-direction, security of the person, and the possibility of unhampered movement. In a contractarian world, the original contractors would wish to ensure that all citizens might enjoy these liberties. In the United States this has been accomplished through the constitutional guarantees of the Bill of Rights and the Fourteenth Amendment.

Full liberty to enjoy and express physical love deserves to be recognized as an additional general good since it, too, develops self-respect. Love in some form is a necessary ingredient of a fulfilled life. Whether this love is for a specific individual, for a number of individuals, or even for an abstract entity, love is essential to what is commonly meant by the meaning of life. In the absence of love, one's life plan is incoherent, the life of the spirit deformed and miserable. Love in its sexual forms affords a uniquely ecstatic experience, for sex makes available to modern men and women experiences increasingly inaccessible in public life: self-transcendence; expression of private fantasy; release of inner tensions; and a socially acceptable expression of the regressive desire to be again an omnipotent child, who is playful, vulnerable, spontaneous, and sensual. While people may choose voluntarily to forgo sex, the coercive prohibition of certain forms of love would be a deprivation of a uniquely significant experience.

Human beings are sexually responsive throughout the year, not just during the period of possible fertilization, as is generally the case with other mammals.[22] Our greater capacity for sensual experience contributes to the distinctively human capability for lasting, profound, personal relationships, because the possibility of ongoing physical love can render a relationship one of continuing delight.[23] Such durable relationships founded on sexual intimacy are happily denominated in the Biblical locution a form of "knowledge," for they proffer a secure disclosure of self, not only through exposure of sexual vulnerabilities but also through the sharing of recesses of the self otherwise remote or inaccessible. It is no accident that these relationships are regarded as fundamentally important. Whom one marries, for example, is generally conceived to be a decision at least as consequential as the choice of occupation. Love expresses itself in the desire to participate with the beloved in caring for common projects created by the relationship, some of which take on a durable character as objects, activities, or even as children who survive the relationship and embody its lasting value. In sum, the glimpses of self that love affords, the mutual shaping of expectations and lifestyles, the communion of aspirations and hopes, all suggest the extraordinary significance in human life of romantic physical love and support further the proposition that freedom to love should be considered a general good.

Love is defined conceptually by its peculiar aims, beliefs, and experiences — e.g., the intensity of the experience (typically, one does not love moderately), the desire to promote the good of another, the identification of another's interests as one's own (experiencing joy when the other is joyful, sadness when the other is sad), the desire for physical and psychological closeness. The concept of love does not imply the form its physical expression must take but comprehends forms of intimacy that express the evident intention of good for another person. Sexual intercourse, for example, enables one to express love through the sharing of pleasure. Short of nonconsensual sadism, which cannot logically exemplify love, there is no ideal or exclusive or proper physical expression of sexual love, for a large and indeterminate class of forms of sexual intercourse are compatible with the aims of love.

These observations illustrate the philosophical error in Augustine's influential model of sexuality. Augustine supposed human sexuality always to be a wild, incoherent, animal passion whose drives undermine human capacities for self-control. He believed that complete self-control would use sexuality only for procreation within marriage and that human beings feel shame over their sexuality when they do not experience sex in the sole proper way. Augustine at once underestimated the peculiarly human capacity for self-command over sexual desire and overestimated the force of sexuality as a kind of dark, ungovernable, Bacchic posession. Human sexuality, as sexologists have emphasized,[24] is, unlike all other comparable biological appetites, malleable and subject to conscious control. Humans can and do postpone sex indefinitely, sometimes for a lifetime. They engage in sexual intercourse for diverse purposes — to express love, or for recreation, or for procreation. No one purpose necessarily dominates; the purpose chosen depends on context. Augustine and the tradition he fostered neglected to see the distinct ways in which humans can regulate their sexual lives. Failing to understand the intrinsic human competence to control one's sexual life, he deemed unnatural a most natural use of sexuality, namely, as an illustration of love and recreation between two people. If anything, the distinctive mark of natural human sexuality is that it is not narrowly tied to reproduction. From this perspective, we can see that the Augustinian idea that procreation is the only proper sexual function is, at best, a plausible description of the animal, not the human, world. A more exact use of the "natural-unnatural" distinction would be to call the exclusive use of sex for procreation unnatural for humans, though natural for animals. Thus, sexual relations between same-sexed partners should not be included within the notion of "unnatural acts"; homosexuality is not necessarily an impairment of proper function.

I will now introduce these meditations on love into a contractarian model of ethics. As I have suggested, the contractors in the original position would regard self-respect as the primary good. Accordingly, their focus would be on moral principles that ensure that people have the maximum opportunity to attain self-respect. Under such principles, people would not be constrained to love or not to love, nor to love in certain ways and not in others, nor to love with certain consequences but not others. Freedom to love would mean that a mature individual might have autonomy to decide how or whether to love another. Restrictions on the form of love, imposed in the name of the distorting rigidities of convention possessing no relation to individual emotional capacities and needs, would be condemned. Individual autonomy in matters of love would ensure the growth of people who call their emotional natures their own, secure in the development of attachments that bear the mark of spontaneous human feeling and that touch personal original impulses. In contrast, restrictions on individual autonomy starve one's emotional capacities, withering individual feeling into conventional gesture and strong native pleasures into vicarious fantasies.

As the occasion to express love is an important element in the full realization of self-respect, social institutions such as marriage should be arranged so that people are accorded fair opportunity to form love relationships according to their desires and to receive whatever institutional recognition is necessary to perfect such relationships. Logically, the following principle of justice should be incorporated in the contractarian "original position":

The principle of love as a civil liberty

Basic institutions are to be arranged so that every person is guaranteed the greatest liberty, opportunity, and capacity to love, compatible with a like liberty, opportunity, and capacity for all.

The derivation of this principle, being a specification of the more general principles of justice, depends on the preliminary assumption that the contractors are ignorant of their particular desires, nature, and circumstances and therefore cannot look to religious duties of procreation to override the liberty to love. Nor can there be any appeal to a taste or distaste for certain forms of physical love in order to override the equal liberty to love. Rather, the contractors' reasoning in the original position will depend wholly on empirical inference and knowledge. Arguments based on perceptions and intuitions not admissible in the original position must be rejected.

In the light of contemporary understanding of the status of sexuality in human life, a single principle has evolved from the more general moral principles underlying the constitutional constraints on the authority of the majority to make laws. This, the idea of love as a civil liberty qualified by limiting moral principles of nonmaleficence, fidelity, paternalism, etc., is, I believe, the fundamental ethic supporting the constitutional right to privacy. We must now apply this analysis to consensual homosexual acts.

III. THE CONSTITUTIONALITY OF LAWS PROHIBITING UNNATURAL ACTS

The majority opinion in *Doe,* affirmed by the Supreme Court, found allegedly unnatural acts, even those between consenting adults in the privacy of their homes, to be outside the protection of the constitutional right to privacy. An understanding of the moral status and weight of the right, in light of the theory of justice described in this chapter, compels a conclusion contrary to that of the Court. There are convincing moral and constitutional reasons why putatively unnatural acts of the kind involved in *Doe* should indeed be accorded the protection of the constitutional right to privacy.

1. The Unnatural and the Principle of Equal Liberty

We begin with the opinions of Justices Harlan and Goldberg, in *Poe* v. *Ullman*[25] and *Griswold* v. *Connecticut*[26] respectively, cited by the district court in *Doe* as the foundation of its holding that the constitutional right to privacy is limited to marital relationships and does not include "deviant" sexual conduct. In fact, as Judge Merhige shows in his dissent,[27] opinions subsequent to *Griswold* found the constitutional right to privacy applicable in non-marital contexts.[28] If the right to privacy extends to sex among unmarried couples or even to autoeroticism, it is impossible to understand how the Court could justifiably decline to consider fully the application of this right to private, consensual, non-conforming sex acts.

The Court might distinguish between heterosexual and homosexual forms of sexual activity, but can this distinction be defended rationally? Ultimately, such a view rests on the belief that homosexual behavior is unnatural and is to be excluded altogether from the scope of the constitutional right to privacy, just as the obscene is excluded from the first amendment protection.[29] However, an analysis of the application of the notion of the "unnatural" to deviant sexual acts, and an examination of the moral force of the constitutional right to privacy, compel rejection of the Court's view.

The use of so imprecise a notion as "the unnatural" to distinguish between those acts not protected by the constitutional right to privacy and those which are protected is clearly unacceptable. The case in which the constitutional right to privacy originated involved contraception—a practice that the Augustinian would deem unnatural. (In the Augustinian view, the use of contraceptives, abortifacients, or pornography is unnatural, because such practices frustrate the essential connection between sexual experience and procreation. Victorian physicians wrote of the weak, scrofulous, and even monstrous children who resulted from the use of contraceptives in the home;[30] homosexuality, similarly, was perceived as a kind of distorting nervous disorder.[31] Apparently, the Court concluded that the "unnaturalness" of contraception or of abortion is constitutionally inadmissible and cannot limit the scope of the right to privacy. The very origin of the right to privacy as a morally necessary constitutional concept arose from the Court's just perception that the use of the notion of the unnatural in limited, personal, sexual liberty was inconsistent with basic constitutional values of personal liberty.

The Court's implicit rejection of the view that contraception and abortion are unnatural reflects a considered contemporary attitude, for there is no empirical evidence that these practices are, necessarily, damaging to body or soul. On the contrary, many people believe that contraception affords a humane and desirable way to regulate the consequences of sexual activity. Contraception, by demarcating the use of sexuality as an expression of love from the use of sexuality for procreation, broadens the range of choices available to men and women.

In considering the constitutionality of allowing the notions of the majority about what is unnatural to limit the right to privacy, the Court must take into account two crucial variables: (1) the lack of evidence that these practices are, in any sense to which empirical data are relevant, unnatural; and (2) the growing contemporary understanding that people should have the maximum liberty to love. The enforcement of the majority's prejudices, without any plausible empirical basis, could be independently unconstitutional as a violation of due process rationality in legislation. To enforce popular but personal tastes in matters involving fair access to love would violate a fundamental human right. The moral theory of the Constitution, built as a bulwark against "serious oppressions of the minor party in the community,"[32] requires that such moral rights be upheld and protected against the prejudices of the majority. The contractarian theory provides the moral basis for these constitutional protections by emphasizing each individual's right to a greatest equal liberty, opportunity, and capacity to love, compatible with a like liberty, opportunity, and capacity for all.

The personal beliefs of the majority are also inadmissible in a constitutional assessment of laws prohibiting forms of sexual "deviance" between consenting adults in private. There is no generally acceptable empirical evidence that homosexuality is unnatural. Many cultures that have other notions of what is unnatural do not regard homosexuality as unnatural. Individuals within our own culture who find certain acts unnatural (e.g., torturing one's children) have argued, on the basis of facts unknown to or misunderstood by the traditional view, that homosexuality is not unnatural. For example, it is now known that homosexuality is part of our mammalian heritage. Many societies (as did ancient Greece) include homosexuality among legitimate sexual conduct, and some prescribe it in the form of institutional pederasty. There is no apparent distinction between the heterosexual and homosexual populations in terms of symptoms of mental illness or measures of self-esteem and self-acceptance. In general, apart from their sexual preference, exclusively homosexual people are indistinguishable from the general population. Finally, homosexual preference appears to be a largely irreversible adaptation of natural human propensities to social circumstances at a very early age.[33]

The cumulative impact of such facts is clear. The notion of "unnatural acts," which deviate from a fixed concept of proper sexual functioning and result in damage or degradation, is not properly applied to homosexual acts performed in private between consenting adults. Homosexuality is clearly a natural expression of human sexual competences and sensitivities, and does not reflect any form of damage, decline, or injury. To deny the legitimacy of such love is itself a human evil, a denial of the distinctive capacities of human nature for sensual and loving experience.

As mentioned above, the application of the term "unnatural acts" to sexual deviance grew out of Plato's twin arguments: (1) that homosexual relations between males involved the loss of desirable character traits (e.g., courage and temperance); and (2) that human sexuality has one proper form, namely, procreation. I have already discussed the misconceptions underlying the procreational model. The view that male homosexuality implies the loss of desirable character traits rests on the idea that sexual relations between males reduces one or both parties to the assumedly degraded status of a female. The latter idea betrays an intellectual confusion of sexual preference and gender identity, when in fact there is no correlation between them. Homosexual females or males may be very insistent about their respective gender identities and have quite typical "feminine" or "masculine" personalities. Their homosexuality is defined only by their erotic preference for members of the same biological sex. Furthermore, the notion that women are inferior to men is repugnant to contemporary jurisprudence and morality. If such crude and unjust sexual stereotypes lie at the bottom of anti-homosexuality laws, the stereotypes should be uprooted.

Despite empirical evidence and contemporary reinterpretation of Biblical prohibitions,[34] some religious groups in our society will continue to condemn homosexuality as unnatural, just as they continue to abhor contraception. They acknowledge a religious duty to reproduce, believing that any use of sexuality without the intention and likelihood of procreation is unnatural. These people have a moral right to govern their own personal lives in accordance with their views. However, the imposition of their understanding of sexuality upon society at large is not justifiable on generally acceptable empirical grounds. Religious groups cannot legitimately require that others, who do not share their views, be forbidden to love or to express themselves sexually in the only ways available to them. That views are based on religious perceptions, not mere whim, should not allow them to be thrust upon nonbelievers. Indeed, to the extent that a group's views rest solely on religious perceptions not accessible to ordinary empirical investigation, the imposition of that group's views upon other people violates not only the constitutional right to privacy but the establishment of religion clause of the first amendment.[35]

There is no logically consistent explanation for the Court's refusal to enforce concepts of the "unnatural" in the case of contraception while permitting statutes based on similar concepts to prohibit sexual deviance. Indeed, the moral arguments in the latter case are more compelling. When struck down in *Griswold*, the statutes condemning certain forms of contraception as "unnatural" probably no longer reflected the opinion of the majority. Accordingly, the need for constitutional protection, while proper, was perhaps not exigent. However, in the case of homosexuality, there is good reason to believe that homosexual men and women as a group are subject to exactly the kind of unjust social hatred that constitutional guarantees were designed to combat.[36]

Many forms of murder are quite natural human occurrences, and yet we do not regard them as immune from criminal prosecution. The naturalness of homosexual experience does not in itself legitimize such behavior. We have, however, argued that not only are homosexual acts natural, they also involve the liberty to love, which must, within limits, be morally and constitutionally guaranteed. Indeed, the anti-homosexuality laws represent a more severe incursion on this liberty than do the contested statutes in the other right to privacy cases. Contraception, abortion, and pornography laws do not forbid sexual intimacy altogether; anti-sodomy laws forbid utterly certain forms of the expression of love.

I have argued that the concept of love is marked by certain characteristic goals, beliefs, and experiences that are compatible with several forms of physical expression, both heterosexual and homosexual. To suppose that only heterosexual behavior can be love is to suppose that love has a kind of canonical physical form: a moral error based on conceptual confusion.

The term "unnatural acts" may, no doubt, be applied properly to some kinds of sexual acts, but homosexual acts per se are not among them. Once the deathly pall of the unnatural is lifted from homosexuality, the concept of love can no longer be limited to intercourse between the biological sexes, and we may perceive the prohibition of homosexuality as the moral wrong it is.

The depth of the injustice that these prohibitions inflict can be seen in terms of their effects upon exclusively homosexual individuals and upon their right to fair access to self-respect. First, laws prohibiting homosexual conduct inhibit persons inclined toward this form of sexual activity from obtaining sexual satisfaction in the only way they find natural. Second, these laws encourage blackmail by providing the means by which homosexual men and women can be threatened with exposure or prosecution. Such vulnerability to blackmail may discourage employers from hiring homosexual persons on the ground that the latter are security risks. Third, laws prohibiting consensual, adult, homosexual activity provide grounds for discrimination against homosexual people in employment, housing, and public accommodation.

The cumulative effect of such laws is to deprive homosexual men and women of a secure respect for their own competence to build personal relationships. The degree of emotional sacrifice thus exacted for no defensible reason seems to be one of the most unjust deprivations the law can compel. Persons are deprived of a realistic basis for having confidence and security in their most basic emotional propensities. Criminal penalties, employment risks, and social prejudices converge to render dubious a person's most spontaneous native sentiments—dividing emotions, physical expression, and self-image in a cruelly gratuitous way. The deepest damage is spiritual. A person surrounded by false social and sexual conceptions, which are supported by law, finds it difficult to experience self-esteem in the emotions and in their natural expression. Without such self-esteem love lacks foundation; physical desire, wayward and restless, finds no meaningful or enduring object. Instead of being assured fair access to love, the homosexual individual is driven into a secretive and concealed world of shallow and often anonymous physical encounters.[37] The achievement of emotional relationships of any depth or permanence is made a matter of heroic individual effort when it could, as with heterosexual relations, be part of the warp and woof of ordinary social possibility and opportunity. In forbidding exclusively homosexual men and women to express sexual love in the only way they prefer naturally, the law deprives them of the good in life that love affords.

In terms of both the lack of empirical evidence for applying the label "unnatural act" to homosexual behavior and the intrusion upon individuals' rights to love and self-respect, we can see that the performance of the so-called "unnatural acts" that were involved in *Doe* v. *Commonwealth's Attorney for City of Richmond* should fall within the protection of the constitutional right to privacy articulated in earlier case law. The district court in *Doe* erred both in failing to take into account adequately the implications of the post-*Griswold* Supreme Court privacy cases, and in failing even to note that the issue before the court merited the most exacting constitutional scrutiny. The Supreme Court, in summarily affirming this clearly erroneous opinion, failed to develop underlying constitutional values in a rationally or morally defensible way. Indeed, by neglecting to hear oral argument or to write an opinion on an issue so significant to the preservation of the fundamental constitutional rights of minorities, the Court failed not only to do justice but even to explain itself in the way required by minimal due process in cases of such importance.

2. Equal Liberty and the Protection of Moral Standards

We see, then, that private, consensual, homosexual acts between adults deserve to fall within the protection of the constitutional right to privacy and should be accorded whatever protection is given other forms of love. The relevant constitutional question is whether statutory restrictions on putatively unnatural acts, such as those upheld in *Doe*, are compatible with the underlying constitutional principles of equal liberty, opportunity, and capacity to love, consistent with a like liberty, opportunity, and capacity for all.

Initially, it is important to know how the principle of love as a civil liberty is to be understood. In deriving this principle, we observed that the value of autonomous capacities in matters of love turned on the existence of developed capacities of rational choice. Thus, the principle is not intended to apply to persons, such as children, presumed to lack rational capacities. Nor, is there any objection to the reasonable regulation of obtrusive solicitation of sex nor, of course, to forcible forms of intercourse of any kind.

In addition, we suggest that the scope of the principle of love as a civil liberty is limited by other moral principles, for example: principles of not killing, harming, or inflicting gratuitous cruelty; principles of paternalism in narrowly-defined circumstances; and principles of fidelity.[38] Here are formulated the relevant moral and constitutional principles to permit some reasonable legitimate restrictions on complete individual freedom. The Supreme Court in *Paris Adult Theatre I* v. *Slaton*[39] confirmed this view when it held that the constitutional right to privacy did not require that consenting adults have access to obscene materials in a movie house. Whether or not *Paris* is a correct interpretation of the relation of obscenity law and the first amendment, it recognized that the values of the constitutional right to privacy are largely concerned with the special status of the home as a sanctuary for intimate emotions and relationships.

I agree with the Court's rejection of the view that the law should have altogether no role in enforcing moral principles. There remains the question of whether in *Doe* the Court correctly construed its own principles, i.e., whether statutes of the kind upheld in *Doe* can be justified by any of the principles qualifying the principle of love as a civil liberty, recalling that any restriction upon liberty must be justified on the basis of facts ascertainable by generally acceptable empirical methods.

Statutes, such as those considered in *Doe*, that absolutely prohibit deviant sexual acts cannot be justified consistently with the principles just mentioned. These statutes are not limited to forcible or public forms of sexual intercourse, nor to sexual intercourse by or with children; they extend as well to private consensual acts between adults. To say that such laws are justified because indirectly they stop homosexual intercourse by or with the underaged, would be as absurd as to recommend absolute prohibitions on heterosexual intercourse for the same reason. There are no data proving that homosexual persons as a class are more often involved in offenses with the young than are heterosexual persons. Nor is there any reliable evidence that anti-homosexual laws inhibit children from becoming homosexual. As has been noted, sexual preference is settled, largely irreversibly, in infancy and well before laws could have an effect upon the child. If the state has any legitimate interest in determining the sexual preference of its citizens, that interest cannot constitutionally be secured by overbroad statutes that tread upon the rights of exclusively homosexual persons and by laws that pursue irrationally an object only to be effected by state intervention in the earliest stages of child rearing.[40]

Other moral principles that might qualify the principle of equal liberty to love also fail to justify absolute prohibitions on consensual sexual deviance. Homosexual relations, for example, are not generally violent. Thus, prohibitory statutes could not be justified by moral principles of nonmaleficence. There is no convincing evidence that homosexuality is either harmful to the participant or correlated with any form of mental or physical disease or defect. To the contrary, there is evidence that anti-sodomy laws, which force homosexual men and women into forms of heterosexual marriage unnatural to them or which otherwise distort and disfigure their reasonable pursuit of natural emotional fulfillment, harm the homosexual people and others in deep and permanent ways. Accordingly, principles of legitimate state paternalism do not come into play here.[41]

Empirical support for the view that homosexuality is a kind of degenerative social poison and leads directly to disease, social disorder, or even to natural disaster as Emperor Justinian supposed when condemning homosexuality as a capital offense, would indeed justify anti-homosexual laws.[42] Principles of justice must be compatible with the stability of institutions of social cooperation. In particular, the principle of equal liberty would not extend to forms of liberty incompatible with stable social cooperation. If the above allegations regarding homosexuality were true, homosexual behavior might fairly be prohibited on the grounds that it undermines the entire constitutional order of equal liberties. However, these fears are unjustified. Numerous nations, including many in Western Europe, have long allowed homosexual acts between consenting adults and have suffered no consequent social disorder, disease, disruption, or the like.[43] England recently legalized such acts with no untoward results.[44]

One final argument has been used to justify a general prohibition upon homosexuality—the argument for preserving moral standards, invoked by the district court in *Doe* as "the promotion of morality and decency."[45] That court believed this to be the ultimate rationale for the legitimacy of the Virginia sodomy statute. The argument takes two forms: (1) a general jurisprudential thesis about the relation of law and morals, and (2) an interpretation of the ethics qualifying the principle of love as a civil liberty. Neither view can be sustained.

The classic modern statement of the jurisprudential moral thesis was made by Devlin[46] against Hart,[47] repeating many of the arguments made earlier by Stephen[48] against Mill.[49] The Devlin-Hart debate centered on the jurisprudential interpretation of the Wolfenden Report,[50] which recommended, among other measures, abolishing criminal penalties for homosexual acts between consenting adults. Devlin, in questioning the report, focused on its proposition that certain private immoral acts are not the business of the law. Criminal law, Devlin argued, is completely unintelligible without reference to morality, which it enforces. For example, the fact that two parties had agreed to kill one another does not relieve the killer of criminal liability, for the act in question is immoral. The privacy of the act is irrelevant. Devlin maintains that morality is the necessary condition for the existence of society. To change the law in such a way as to violate that morality is to threaten the stability of the social order. Morality, in this connection, is to be understood in terms of the ordinary person's intuitive sense of right and wrong, as determined, Devlin suggests, by taking a man at random from the Clapham omnibus. Just as we prove the standards of negligence for purposes of civil or criminal liability by appealing to the judgment of ordinary citizens acting as jurors, so can we prove the applicable standards of morality in the same way. Ordinary men and women morally loathe homosexuality; accordingly, homosexuality is immoral and must be forbidden by law.

Superficially, Devlin's argument appears to resemble an acceptable constitutional argument. There should be no objection to prohibiting clearly immoral acts that threaten the existence of society. Further, it is surely very plausible that law and morals have a deep and systematic relation of the kind Devlin suggests. However, these abstractly credible general propositions cannot support the specific argument that Devlin propounds. He argues, probably correctly, that the criminal law arises from the morality that it enforces. But then Devlin falsely identifies morality with conventional social views in a manner that renders unthinkable, if not unintelligible, the whole idea of moral criticism and reform of social convention. Adoption of this view would effectively freeze the measure of legally enforceable moral ideas into an ephemeral victory of one set of contending ideological forces over another. There is no good reason to identify morality with social convention, since the latter is based on an indefensible and naive moral philosophy as well as on unexamined and unsound sociology.

Recent moral philosophy has been increasingly occupied with the clarification of the conceptual structure of ordinary moral reasoning.[51] The concept of morality of ethics is not openly flexible; there are certain determinate constraints on the kind of beliefs that may be counted as moral in nature. Examples of applicable constraints are treating others as you would like to be treated in comparable circumstances; judging the morality of principles by the consequences of their universal application;

and minimization of fortuitous human differences such as clan, caste, ethnicity, or color as a basis for differential treatment. It follows from this conception that a view is not moral simply because it is passionately and sincerely held; nor because it has a certain emotional depth; nor because it is the view of one's father, mother, or clan; nor because it is conventional. On the contrary, a moral point of view affords a way to assess whether any of these beliefs, which may often press one to action, is in fact worthy of ethical commitment.

Thus, moral views of the kind that the law enforces do not rest on mere social convention. They are, rather, marked by a special universalizing kind of reasoning and by an appeal to principles that morally aware persons would defend whether they were helped or injured by those principles. However adequate the contract model of moral principles employed in this chapter, the model does attempt to take these features of moral reasoning seriously; Devlin's theory does not. His argument is based on nonmoral instincts, social tastes, and accepted conventions. It is a mark of the unhappy separation of legal theory from serious moral theory that Devlin's superficial analysis can have been taken so seriously by lawyers, when its moral basis is so transparently inadequate.

Devlin's position is not, however, merely unsatisfactory as theory. If it were accepted, it would be morally repelling in its conclusions. Intransigently resistant to critical moral scrutiny, it would elevate all forms of social prejudice into moral bases for the law, even though unsupported by intelligible reasoning of any kind. It would undermine the entire notion of rational due process of law, which requires that reasons be given in order to justify deprivations of life, liberty, or property. Ultimately, it dignifies blind and possibly vicious prejudice into the moral foundation of law. Instead of defending people from passions born of ignorance, it simply makes those passions the measure of legally enforceable morality.

The attraction of Devlin's theory for judges is its apparent objectivity: Without appeal to subjective considerations,[52] it affords a definite criterion for the morality that the law enforces. However, the empirical objectivity of existing custom has nothing to do with the notions of moral impartiality and objectivity that are, or should be, of judicial concern in determining the public morality that supports the law. The idea that the pursuit of moral objectivity must collapse into dependence upon custom is a confusion of inquiries, arising from an untenable distinction between subjective moral belief and the public morality of the law. There is no such distinction. Views, to be moral, require a certain kind of justification. Judges, in interpreting legally enforceable moral ideas, must appeal to the kind of reasoning that is moral. As judges they do not abdicate their capacity for moral reasoning as persons. On the contrary, competence and articulateness in such reasoning comprise the virtue we denominate judicial.

However, even if Devlin's theory could be defended on theoretical or practical grounds, it must be rejected as incompatible with the moral theory implicit in constitutional order. The Constitution rests on the idea that moral rights of individuals cannot be violated. Accordingly, the Supreme Court has correctly and consistently rejected arguments that question constitutional rights on the basis of popular prejudices, whether the prejudices are racial or sexual.[53] Such prejudices, far from enforced by the Court, have been circumscribed in order to protect constitutional liberties.

We have argued that homosexual love comes within a constitutionally protected right, the right to privacy. The basis for this constitutional right is the moral right of maximum fair access to love. This moral right rests on the premise that, just as mature persons would not want the form in which they feel or express love to be regulated or prohibited, so should they extend similar consideration to others. Accordingly, rather than it being immoral to espouse homosexual behavior, as Devlin argued, it is immoral to prohibit homosexuality. Popular social attitudes that are not based on generally acceptable empirical facts are precisely those forms of sexual prejudice from which people should be protected. To appeal to popular attitudes, as Devlin does, in an attempt to restrict the moral rights of an unpopular minority, is to illustrate the need for the constitutional right to privacy.

Devlin's brand of argument for preserving moral standards is objectionable to moral and constitutional principles. There is, however, another form of the argument that is not similarly objectionable for it rests on an interpretation of the moral principles restricting the principle of love as a civil liberty. The district court in *Doe* employed such a mode of argument when suggesting that the moral issue before it was not that homosexuality is objectionable per se, but rather that, in the present state of society, homosexual behavior tends to evade certain moral principles, e.g., the principles of fidelity found in heterosexual marriage and family obligations.[54] The court's use of the argument is, as we have seen, fundamentally fallacious. There remains the popular belief that homosexuality, if allowed, would violate moral principles implicit in the institution of the heterosexual family.

While this line of thought has the general form of acceptable moral and constitutional arguments, its factual assumptions are utterly undocumented by evidence. For example, the argument makes the unsupported assumption that homosexuality would cause a decline in heterosexual marriages. But, as Judge Merhige indicated in his dissent in *Doe,* such a claim is so flimsy empirically as to be "unworthy of judicial response."[55] Historical and contemporary data show that homosexual relationships are compatible with heterosexual marriage. The numerous countries that have legalized homosexual relations have shown no decline in the rate of heterosexual marriages. It appears that acceptance of homosexual relations has no effect upon heterosexual marriage.[56]

The belief that, if homosexuality were allowed, the heterosexual family would decline, is ancient and pervasive. One striking modern formulation of this notion is that the lifestyle of exclusively homosexual persons does more harm socially than the mere occurrence in private of consensual homosexual acts. To legitimize certain sex acts is to legitimize an undesirable way of life. These sex acts, even in private between consenting adults, may justly be prohibited.

It is important to inquire with care what this intuitive allegation amounts to, for a form of it bears the imprimatur of the Supreme Court itself.[57] The suggestion is that public knowledge of the legitimacy of homosexual acts would undermine the desire by heterosexual men and women to make the personal sacrifices necessary to sustain a way of life supportive of the monogamous nuclear family. The legitimacy of remaining unmarried has not undermined the heterosexual family. Indeed, one form of the legitimate single state, religious celibacy, has long been regarded as sanctified by influential Western religions. Clerical celibacy has not made the heterosexual family less stable. Why, then, should the recognition of homosexuality as a legitimate lifestyle be greeted in a radically different manner? The suggestion must be that homosexual preference is so strong and heterosexual preference so weak (and conventional family life so unattractive) that people would tend to abandon heterosexual marriage if homosexuality were legitimized. As we have seen, there is not a shred of empirical support for this view. Not only is exclusive heterosexuality the preference of an overwhelming majority, but the attractions of heterosexual marriage are deep-seated and permanent features of the human condition. Human beings, generally raised in a nuclear heterosexual family, naturally regard the cooperation and creative sharing that typify the heterosexual family as the answer, or part of the answer, to the recurrent human problems of loneliness and isolation. For most people, conventional marriage will remain the standard answer to the metaphysics of the meaning of life, by supplying a natural solution to human needs for sexual release, intimacy, and the desire for immortality through child-rearing. It is a bizarre underestimation of the attractions of family life to suppose that to legitimize homosexuality as a way of life would detract from the family at all. Even in this era of growing sexual freedom and rising divorce rates, there is no sign that heterosexual marriage as an institution is in general less attractive. The divorce rates show not a distaste for marriage but only less willingness to stick with the original partners in marriage. The important and striking feature of this phenomenon is that divorced people typically remarry; they reject their previous partner, not the institution of marriage itself.[58]

As the "way of life" argument lacks factual content, it must depend for its force upon a kind of hysterical sexual fantasy regarding the pervasive and deadly attractions of homosexuality. That argument cannot be sustained as an empirical proposition, even though it can be understood as the unmistakable psychological residue of fear and loathing left by the long tradition that condemned nonprocreative sex as unnatural. The theory that legitimate homosexuality will destroy the family is circular and should have no force independent of the empirical assumptions on which it rests. Undoubtedly, residues of guilt and fear remain long after we reject, on rational grounds, the beliefs supporting those guilts and fears. This psychological truth, however, does not validate regressive emotions as a legitimate basis for law. If reason requires us to reject these negative emotions as a basis for ethical conduct, the morality of law can require no less.

It is difficult to understand how the state has the right, on moral grounds, to protect heterosexual love at the expense of homosexual love. Contractarian principles seem to forbid precisely such a sacrifice of the fundamental interests of one group in order to secure the greater happiness of other groups or of the whole. Contractarian principles prescribe minimal benchmarks of human decency, which rest on boundary constraints respecting the interest of all persons equally in general goods and which limit the power of majority rule to plough under the interest of minorities.

Surely there is no constitutional or moral duty to marry or, more generally, to procreate. Such an idea violates everything that the constitutional right to privacy was designed to protect: namely, autonomy to decide whether and how to love. People have children for reasons determined by their personal notions of happiness and fulfillment; they perform no moral duty, nor are they morally admirable, by having children. Indeed, in the present state of overpopulation, many suppose and argue that there are moral duties not to procreate.[59]

Finally, there is reason to believe that the argument for protecting marriage and the family is proposed hypocritically. If the argument were meant seriously, state laws against fornication and adultery would be pressed as vigorously as the anti-homosexuality laws. But, in many states, such laws either do not exist or penalize homosexuality much more severly than heterosexual offenses.[60] This suggests that anti-homosexuality laws rest not on rational arguments consistently pursued but on ancient prejudice and a vestige of ideas of unnatural conduct.

The argument for preserving moral standards is circular: Homosexuality is considered immoral and prohibiting it is, therefore, moral. We have argued, however, that laws against homosexuality violate the moral right of people to be treated as persons with fair access to love and self-respect. It is not homosexuality that is immoral, rather the anti-homosexuality laws themselves, for they perpetuate injustice through traditional prejudice born of indefensible fear.

Everyone in our civilization praises love, but a particular form of love between parties of the same sex transmogrified unrecognizably by popular imagination from its natural simplicity into an unnatural picture of degradation and exploitation, has been made the butt of social ridicule and the object of criminal punishment. The Supreme Court's summary affirmance in *Doe* reflects popular imagination and truncates abruptly the reach of constitutional rights, in horror at "unnatural acts." In *Doe*, the Court failed to develop constitutional values in a reasonable way. Instead of showing how constitutional values, popularly accepted in the area of contraception, apply equally to unjustly hated minorities, the Court acquiesced in unexamined popular bromides and shabby arguments unworthy of our constitutional tradition.

FOOTNOTES

1. 425 U.S. 901 (1976), aff'g without opinion 403 F. Supp. 1199 (E.D. Va. 1975) (three-judge court).
2. See Richards, "Unnatural Acts and the Constitutional Right to Privacy: A Moral Theory," 45 *Ford. L. Rev.* 1281 (1977) (herinafter "Unnatural Acts"); see also Richards, *The Moral Criticism of Law*, Dickenson Pub. Co., Inc.: Encino, California 1977, at 77-109. The present article is a condensed redaction of "Unnatural Acts." In addition to the omission of much of the more purely legal and jurisprudential parts of the original article, I have chosen to omit entirely most of the extensive exploratory footnotes of the original article. Occasionally, I have inserted cross-references to these notes, but I have not done so systematically. My intention here is to sketch the broad outlines of the argument of "Unnatural Acts." Any reader interested in pursuing the argument should consult the original, especially with respect to background notes. See also Richards, "Sexual Autonomy and the Constitutional Right to Privacy: A Case Study in Human Rights and the Unwritten Constitution," *30 Hastings L.J.* 957 (1979).
3. See, for example, Ulysses' speech of hierarchical order. W. Shakespeare, "Troilus and Cressida", act I, scene iii.
4. Of a subject's judging his king, Shakespeare wrote: "O, forfend it, God, that in a Christian climate, souls refin'd should show so heinous, black, obscene a deed!", W. Shakespeare, "Richard II", act IV, scene i.
5. The theory of the unnatural here employed was collaboratively developed with Donald Levy, Brooklyn College (Philosophy). The theory is developed at greater and more convincing length in Donald Levy, "Perversion and the Unnatural as Moral Categories", *Ethics* (forthcoming).
6. See Plato, *Laws* Book VIII, 835d-842a.
7. Aristotle, *Politics* 1257a-1258b.
8. This phrase appears in Catholic theological commentaries on the obscene and unnatural. See, e.g., Gardiner, "Moral Principles Towards a Definition of the Obscene," 20 *Law & Contemp. Prob.* 560, 567 (1955).
9. See Augustine, 1 *The City of God* 470-72 (M. Dods Trans. 1950).

64

10. "(T)his lust, of which we at present speak, is the more shameful on this account, because the soul is there neither master of itself, so as not to lust at all, nor of the body, so as to keep the members under control of the will; for if it were thus ruled, there would be no shame." Augustine, 2 *The City of God* 40 (M. Dods trans. 1948).

11. *Summa Theologica* II-II, Q. cliv. I, II, and XII.

12. 4 W. Blackstone, *Commentaries* *215.

13. 381 U.S. 479 (1965).

14. 394 U.S. 557 (1969).

15. *Id.* at 564.

16. 405 U.S. 438 (1972).

17. 405 U.S. at 453 (emphasis in original).

18. 410 U.S. 113 (1973).19.

19. *Stanley v. Georgia,* 394 U.S. 557, 546 (1969), quoting *Olmstead v. United States,* 277 U.S. 438, 478 (1928) (Brandeis, J., dissenting).

20. *Paris Adult Theatre I v. Slaton,* 413 U.S. 49, 66 n. 13 (1973).

21. See Richards, *The Moral Criticism of Law,* Dickenson Pub. Co., Inc.: Encino, California 1977.

22. See C. Ford & F. Beach, *Patterns of Sexual Behavior* 199-267 (1951).

23. See I. Eibl-Eibesfeldt, *Love and Hate* 155-69 (1972).

24. See W. Masters & V. Johnson, *Human Sexual Inadequacy* 10 (1970): "Seemingly, many cultures and certainly many religions have risen and fallen on their interpretation and misinterpretation of one basic physiological fact. Sexual functioning is a natural physiological process, yet it has a unique facility that no other natural physiological process, such as respiratory, bladder, or bowel function, can imitate. *Sexual responsivity can be delayed indefinitely or functionally denied for a lifetime.* No other basic physiological process can claim such malleability of physical expression."

25. 367 U.S. 497, 553 (1961) (Harlan, J., dissenting)

26. 381 U.S. 479, 498-99 (1965) (Goldberg, J., dissenting)

27. 403 F. Supp. at 1203-04 (Merhige, J., dissenting)

28. See *Roe v. Wade,* 410 U.S. 113 (1973) (abortion); cf. *Eisenstadt v. Baird,* 405 U.S. 438 (1972) (contraceptives and the unmarried); *Stanley* v. *Georgia,* 394 U.S. 557 (1969) (private use of pornography).

29. For a criticism of this exclusion, see Richards, "Free Speech and Obscenity Law: Toward a Moral Theory of the First Amendment," 123 *U. Pa. L. Rev.* 45 (1974).

30. See J. Haller & R. Haller, *The Physician and Sexuality in Victorian America* 114-15 (1974).

31. See R. von Krafft-Ebing, *Psychopathia Sexualis* 286-350 (12th ed. New York 1950) (1st ed. Leipzig 1901).

32. *The Federalist* No. 78, at 359 (Hallowell ed. 1857) (A. Hamilton)

33. For pertinent background notes supporting the propositions of this paragraph, see Richards, "Unnatural Acts," at 1325-1328, nn. 238-247.

34. See "Unnatural Acts," at 1294-1295, n. 62.

35. See Henkin, "Morals and the Constitution: The Sin of Obscenity", 63 *Colum. L. Rev.* 391 (1963).

36. See "Unnatural Acts," at 1330-1331, n. 265.

37. See L. Humphreys, *Tearoom Trade* 1-15 (1970); M. Hoffman, *The Gay World* ch. 6 (1968).

38. See "Unnatural Acts" and notes cited therein, at 1312-1313.

39. 413 U.S. 49, 57, 66 (1973).

40. For supporting notes, see "Unnatural Acts," 1334-1335, nn. 281-284.

41. For supporting notes, see "Unnatural Acts," 1335, nn. 285-288.

42. See *Id.,* at 1295, n. 66.

43. See W. Barnett, *Sexual Freedom and the Constitution*, at 293, 305-07 (1973).
44. Sexual Offenses Act, 1967, c. 60.
45. 403 F. Supp. 1199, 1202 (E.D. Va. 1975), aff'd without opinion, 425 U.S. 901 (1976).
46. See P. Devlin, *The Enforcement of Morals* (1965).
47. See H.L.A. Hart, *Law, Liberty and Morality* (1963).
48. J. Stephn, *Liberty, Equality, Fraternity*, 135-78 (1967).
49. J.S. Mill, *On Liberty*, in *The Philosophy of John Stuart Mill* (M. Cohen ed. 1961) at 271-93.
50. Report of the Committee on Homosexual Offenses and Prostitution, Report Comnd. No. 247 (1957).
51. See K. Baier, *The Moral Point of View* 187-213 (1958); D. Gauthier, *Practical Reasoning* (1963); G. Grice, *The Grounds of Moral Judgment* 1-35 (1967); R. Hare, *The Language of Morals* (1952); R. Hare, *Freedom and Reason* 86-185 (1963); J. Rawls, *A Theory of Justice* (1971); D.A.J. Richards, *A Theory of Reasons for Action* (1971).
52. See B. Cardozo, *The Nature of the Judicial Process* 108-11, 112, 131, 136 (1949).
53. See, e.g., *Roe v. Wade*, 410 U.S. 113 (1973) (abortion); *Eisenstadt v. Barid*, 405 U.S. 438 (1972) (contraception for unmarried persons); *Loving v. Virginia*, 338 U.S. 1 (1967) (miscegenation); *Griswold v. Connecticut*, 381 U.S. 479 (1965) (contraception); *Brown v. Board of Education*, 347 U.S. 483 (1954) (segregated education).
54. 403 F. Supp. at 1202.
55. 403 F. Supp. at 1205 (Merhige, J. dissenting).
56. For background notes, see "Unnatural Acts" at 1341, nn. 320-322.
57. See *Paris Adult Theatre I v. Slaton*, 413 U.S. 49 (1973).
58. See, generally, M. Bane, *Here to Stay* (1976).
59. See "Unnatural Acts," at 1344, n. 328.
60. See statutes cited in Note, "The Constitutionality of Laws Forbidding Private Homosexual Conduct," 72 *Mich. L. Rev.* 1613, 1622-23 nn. 63-67 (1974).

EMPLOYMENT DISCRIMINATION LAW AND THE RIGHTS OF GAY PERSONS

Judith M. Hedgpeth, J.D.

Any attempt to study employment discrimination based on sexual or affectional preference must recognize the paradoxical and contradictory response by the judicial system to such discrimination. Until very recently the courts casually rejected challenges to discrimination on these grounds and staunchly affirmed the right of government and of the private sector to eliminate "immoral" influences from the work force. The courts consistently echoed the cultural norms of that majority to impose its views on all of society. Early attempts to include gay persons within the recognized constitutional protections offered other cultural, religious, or racial minorities met uniformly with failure. The legal community is now slowly recognizing the need to work to correct this pattern, with much of the effort being led by gay activist attorneys in cooperation with more traditional civil libertarian groups.

Historically, the federal government has provided greater job protection to minorities than have state governments or private industry. Until recently however, no protection at all was given to those discriminated against because of their sexual orientation. The women's and gay liberation movements have helped to expose the extent to which that discrimination has affected the employment opportunities of lesbians and gay men. For many of us, an open affirmation of our lifestyle has spelled the almost automatic loss of our jobs or opportunities for promotion. Those who elect to stay "in the closet" frequently find their jobs jeopardized by rumors that they are "gay", as have those who do not fit the stereotype of the masculine man or the feminine woman. Today this discrimination is under vigorous open attack. At the same time, countervailing forces are working actively for even more discriminatory laws or for stricter enforcement of present ones.

"Sexual orientation" has not yet been added to the protected list of any federal or state nondiscrimination law, although lobbying and educa-

Ms. Hedgpeth graduated with a B.S. in Nursing Science from Arizona State University College of Nursing in 1962 and received her J.D., in 1977, from the Arizona State University College of Law. Precinct committee-person for three years in Arizona, she is currently active in the Lesbian Caucus of the (Arizona) National Organization of Women. All correspondence should be directed to the author, 540 Castro Street, San Francisco, California 94114.

tional efforts are being directed towards this end in Congress and several states. The 1970's saw passage of many local ordinances protecting not only the employment opportunities of homosexual persons, but our rights to housing and public accommodation as well. Repeal efforts during the past two years cast doubt on the effectiveness of that protection. Repeal of gay civil rights ordinances in Dade county, Florida; Wichita, Kansas; St. Paul, Minnesota; and Eugene, Oregon resulted from a full-scale attack by various conservative, religious, and political groups under the leadership of Anita Bryant and Senator John Briggs.

This article will discuss the response by the judicial system to the issue of employment protection for homosexual men and women and will chart present trends in local and state legislative activity. Of equal importance, though not fully examined here, is the recent increase in efforts by the private sector to eliminate discriminatory practices. Since 1970, many private companies, professional organizations, and unions have adopted policies disclaiming and deploring discrimination based on sexual orientation. In practice, such policies have had varied results — and indeed are frequently ignored by those controlling jobs and tenure. However, the development and formalization of these nondiscriminatory practices and goals does create a basis for attacking specific instances of discrimination. The possible uses of these policies to provide an intracorporate private ground for challenging discrimination needs to be explored.

I. PROTECTION AT THE FEDERAL LEVEL

The federal courts have offered considerable protection to minority groups alleging discrimination in public or private employment. Federal litigation protects those discriminated against on the basis of "age, color, race, religion, sex, physical handicap, or nation origin."[1] The creation of the Equal Employment Opportunity Commission has enriched the basic legislative tools with extensive regulations designed to enforce a policy of nondiscrimination toward those minorites. A review of the laws and decisions reveals, however, that the right to equal employment opportunity, fundamental as that right is, has not yet been extended in a meaningful way to workers known to be, or assumed to be, homosexual.

The earliest federal cases dealing with sexual orientation discrimination were brought as challenges to the Federal Civil Service Commission's policy against employing any homosexual person. Until 1965, courts reviewing these regulations consistently sustained the validity of such discrimination. In that year, a federal appeals court in Washington, DC held that the Civil Service Commission must prove just *how* the particular "immoral conduct" of the applicant would affect the ability to perform the work.[2] Although it did not establish a constitutional right of homosexual persons to hold federal employment, this was the first time a federal court seriously questioned discrimination based on sexual preference.

In the 1969 case of *Norton* v. *Macy*,[3] the court held that a fully qualified and competent employee could not be dismissed from federal employment solely on the basis of their homosexuality. The court ruled that there had to be "some reasonably foreseeable, specific connection ('nexus') between an employee's potentially embarrassing conduct and the efficiency of the service." The court declared that homosexual behavior *could* properly be a factor in determining fitness for federal employment and described ways in which homosexual conduct, in the view of the court, might bear on "the efficiency of the service." *Norton* marks the beginning of what has become, in the lower federal courts, a positive shift in the judicial bias. However, some federal courts have not followed the *Norton* guidelines and have perpetuated the view that homosexuality in itself establishes unfitness for employment.

In a decision rendered shortly after *Norton*, the Court of Claims upheld the firing of an Army Office of Transportation employee, stating:[4]

Any schoolboy knows that a homosexual act is immoral, indecent, lewd, and obscene. Adult persons are even more conscious that this is true. If activities of this kind are allowed to be practiced in a government department, it is inevitable that the efficiency of the service will in time be adversely affected.

The language of the decision implies the activity took place on the job, when in fact it occurred in the privacy of the defendant's home, with consenting adults. The judicial bias evident in the opinion reflects a recurrent attitude that homosexual conduct is scandalous and disgraceful, requiring punitive executive policies. Courts rejecting *Norton* have acted on the unacknowledged assumption that homosexuality is equivalent to unfitness and have seen no need to prove any relationship between the capabilities of the individual and the agency's reasons for disqualification. Such judicial reasoning appears to be ceding to decisions that sustain the requirements of the standard delineated in *Norton*. In 1973, a landmark class action suit successfully challenged the Civil Service policy of blanket exclusion of homosexual persons from federal employment. In *Society for Individual Rights* v. *Hampton (S.I.R.)*,[5] the court enjoined the Commission from excluding or discharging an individual solely because that person is homosexual or on the ground that employment of homosexual men and women could bring the service into public contempt. Although the court held that the Civil Service policy was too broad, it left open the possibility that homosexual conduct might justify dismissal where interference with government efficiency could be substantiated with specificity.

While the decision in *S.I.R.* resulted in a laudatory revision of Civil Service guidelines and regulations,[6] the practical effect of the new policy is not yet clear. A recent case raises the fear that the Service could continue its earlier discriminatory practices, by reliance on a provision that covers "infamous or notoriously disgraceful conduct." According to the language of that section, such conduct "implies behavior which is outside the normal pattern and is generally unacceptable in our society." Further definitions suggest that "notoriously disgraceful conduct is that conduct which is shameful in nature and is generally known and talked of in a scornful manner." While the guidelines explicitly provide that individuals cannot be disqualified solely on the basis of their homosexuality, the language makes it clear that the revised guidelines do not offer substantive protections to the lesbian or gay man who is active politically or socially. The standards appear to rely on the reactions of the community or of co-workers to the status, as well as to the specific behavior, of the individual. The language of the opinion in *S.I.R.* suggests that "embarrassment" to a government agency *could* support denial of employment to homosexual persons, even if the embarrassment arose from unreasonable public prejudice. Under present social and political conditions, such a standard gives little security to those who choose to be open about their lifestyle. The opinion does not specify what standard will be used to define "embarrassment" and to what degree the embarrassment must be tolerated by the agency involved before reaching the threshold sufficient to sustain dismissal.

In a case decided three years after *S.I.R.*, the court in *Singer* v. *U.S. Civil Service Commission*[7] accepted the Commission's argument that public statements by a federal employee, clearly directed toward educating others and gaining recognition of the civil liberties of homosexual persons, could justify dismissal under the revised standards. The court failed to find any protected speech, viewing such advocacy as public "flaunting" of the employee's lifestyle. Purporting to apply the *Norton* test, the court in *Singer* found a sufficient *"nexus"* for sustaining Singer's discharge.

This rationale would apparently require gay federal employees to sacrifice their freedoms of speech and association in order to achieve job security. Clearly, the court was strongly influenced by the possibility of adverse public opinion, while evidence as to competence on the job received little consideration. On motion of the Solicitor General, the United States Supreme Court remanded the case to the Commission for reconsideration under the new guidelines. The Commission then upheld Singer's 1972 firing. However, the Appeals Review Board reversed, on the ground that there was:

no evidence which could support a conclusion that the apellant's conduct has in any manner impeded the efficiency of the EEOC . . . We are inclined to agree that

for the most part, the general public does not approve of this type of behavior . . .
this fact, in and of itself, does not show that the EEOC could not effectively and
efficiently carry out its mission as long as the appellant was employed there.[8]

The Review Board based its conclusion on the fact that the EEOC, in
failing to provide evidence supporting the allegation that Singer's behavior as an openly gay person would impair administrative effectiveness,
had, therefore, incorrectly applied its own suitability standards. It remains
to be seen whether a contrary result might be reached if the EEOC were to
present specific proof that the sexual preference of an individual had an
adverse effect on other employees. The "adverse effect argument" was not
successful when raised by the Navy in a discrimination suit brought by a lesbian naval officer.[9]

Federal judicial response to suits involving public school employees has
also resulted in contradictory and inconsistent decisions. While procedural due process (the right to pre-dismissal notice and a hearing) is accorded public employees who possess a valid claim of entitlement to employment, granting a hearing does not guarantee that the employee will
receive a fair or impartial review of their record as a teacher. Homosexual
employees are often dismissed on the basis of substantive standards that
permit disqualification for "immoral or unprofessional conduct" or
"moral turpitude," the most common grounds for discipline when noncriminal behavior is at issue. No case challenging employment disqualification of homosexual persons on the basis of these vague statutes and
policies has thus far been granted review by the United States Supreme
Court. The Court's failure to decide whether private, adult, consensual,
homosexual conduct falls within the constitutional "right to privacy"[10]
leads to further confusion and disagreement in the lower courts. This explains in large part the uneven results in the courts.

Because popular mythology links the homosexual individual with the
child molester, public schoolteachers face a particularly invidious type of
discrimination. Revocation of the teaching credential has been the rule
when a teacher has been convicted of a homosexual "offense".[11] Almost
without exception, these revocations have been upheld by the courts.

Federal courts have generally been more receptive than state courts to
constitutionally based challenges to the loss of school employment for
reasons of sexual preference. An injunction issued by a federal district
court, in *McConnell* v. *Anderson*,[12] barred the University of Minnesota
from rejecting a gay activist as a librarian. The court held that a prospective employee's private life should not be of concern to an employer unless
it could be shown to affect the employee's efficiency in the performance
of employment responsibilities. The injunction was subsequently dissolved
by the Court of Appeals, which cited the "interference" rationale and the
broad discretionary authority vested in the University.[13] The University's
argument that McConnell's activist role would "foist tacit approval of this

socially repugnant concept upon his employer," was accepted by the court. The decision infers that homosexual employees are to be tolerated only if they are willing, and able, to conceal their homosexuality.

A more liberal view was expressed by the Fourth Circuit Court of Appeals in *Acanfora* v. *Board of Education*.[14] There the court extended constitutional protection to Acanfora's public appearances, but sustained his dimissal as a teacher and subsequent placement in a nonteaching position because of his failure to list his affiliation with homophile organizations on his employment application. In the court's view this "deliberate omission" left Acanfora without standing to challenge the constitutionality of the school district's refusal to hire homosexual men and women. The court refused to deal with the underlying reality: Had Acanfora given the information, he would have been denied employment, probably without ever knowing why. This approach requires that gay teachers avoid any involvement in public or political activity in order to retain their teaching positions. Even the trial court in *Acanfora*, which resoundingly declared that "(t)he time has come today for private, consenting, adult homosexuality to enter the sphere of a constitutionally protectable interest," declined to reinstate Acanfora because of the "sensationalism" surrounding his public appearances.

Reinstatement has been considered the appropriate remedy in numerous decisions where public employees have been discharged for exercising rights of free speech on issues outside the area of gay rights. Although this remedy was not granted in *Aumiller* v. *University of Delaware*,[15] the court language indicates judicial recognition of the plantiff's free speech rights. Aumiller, a nontenured lecturer in the Department of Drama, was quoted in a series of local news articles dealing with homosexuality. The resulting publicity was regarded by the administration as reflecting negatively on the University. Following a series of private interviews between the University president and Aumiller, the president decided not to sign a new year's contract for Aumiller, and the University rejected Aumiller's grievance petition.

The court, after careful review of the evidence, awarded compensatory damages to Aumiller for lost employment during the pendency of the litigation and for the emotional distress, embarrassment, and humiliation he had suffered because of the University's actions. A further award of punitive damages against the university president personally, suggests the court's recognition of the need to curb unbridled personal bias on the part of employers. The case certainly marks a new, more humane response to the private and professional damage suffered by gay teachers.

A similar decision was reached in Oregon where a schoolteacher was dismissed because, when questioned by the principal, she admitted she was lesbian. Her lesbianism was entirely private. The evidence introduced in her discrimination suit against the school district established that she was a satisfactory teacher who had never been accused of any "immoral or criminal" acts. Even though it declared unconstitutionally vague the statute that allowed dismissal for "immorality," the court did not reinstate the teacher but simply awarded damages.[16] The rationale for the court's decision was expressed as a balancing between the teacher's interest in completing her one-year employment contract and the possible disruption of the school if she were allowed to do so. The legitimacy of balancing community reaction against an individual's constitutional rights was questioned by dissenting Circuit Judge Lumbard, who observed:

If community resentment was a legitimate factor to consider, few Southern school districts would have been integrated . . . One of the major purposes of the Constitution is to protect individuals from the tyranny of the majority. That purpose would be completely subverted if we allowed the feelings of the majority to determine the remedies available to a member of a minority group who has been the victim of unconstitutional actions.[17]

It is evident that the federal courts disagree on what, if any, protection against employment discrimination should be afforded gay persons. At present, there seems to be consensus on the impermissibility of disqualifying an educator solely on the basis of the status of homosexuality. Differences of opinion center primarily on the basis and scope of a gay teacher's constitutionally protectable interests and on the breadth of discretion enjoyed by school boards in determining whether the exercise of these interests might in some way interfere with the educational system.

Although the courts apparently accept the principle that employment may not be conditioned on the waiver of one's First Amendment rights, they have provided few guidelines for the teacher who seeks to learn the point beyond which out-of-classroom speech justifies dismissal. The threat that a board might find particular speech or opinion "notorious" in retrospect, exerts a chilling effect on the exercise of First Amendment rights. Similarly, to exercise due process rights (by appealing a dimissal) might itself give rise to publicity or community resentment and be interpreted as interfering with the efficiency of a school district, precluding reinstatement. The end result of utilizing community reactions as the justification for dismissal is sure defeat for the gay teacher attempting to exercise constitutional rights of free expression.

II. STATE LEGISLATIVE AND JUDICIAL RESPONSE

State governments, including the judiciary, are increasingly being looked to for protection of civil and constitutional rights. Although gender-based discrimination has not been condemned as severely as racial discrimination by the United States Supreme Court, the California Supreme Court has held that sex, like race, is a "suspect classification" under the State constitution.[18] Defining a group as "suspect" shifts the burden of proof to a higher standard and requires the state to demonstrate a *compelling* (rather than a "rational") interest in continuing to discriminate between members of the class and others similarly situated. Many state and local legislative bodies have responded with statutes and ordinances prohibiting job discrimination by government agencies, by those contracting with or receiving aid from the government, and, in some cases, by private employers. The New York Human Rights Law, as an example, provides:

The state has the responsibility to act to assure that every individual *within this state is afforded an equal opportunity to enjoy a full and productive life and that the failure to provide such equal opportunity, whether because of discrimination, prejudice, or intolerance . . . not only threatens the rights and proper privileges of its inhabitants, but menaces the institutions and foundation of a free democratic state.*[19]

All professions that have licensing statutes and standards have occasionally been the subject of cases involving the licensing of homosexual applicants. In *McLaughlin* v. *Board of Medical Examiners*,[20] a physician arrested for "sexual solicitation" was placed on disciplinary probation and ordered to remain under a psychiatrist's care. The appellate court upheld the order, although its reasoning is directly contrary to that of *Jack M.*, a case involving a California teacher, discussed *infra*.

Attorneys have been the subject of two recent reported decisions. In *In re Kimball*,[21] the New York Court of Appeals held that a 1955 sodomy conviction did not automatically disqualify a 1973 bar applicant, and in *In re Eimers*[22] the Florida Supreme Court held that the status of homosexual orientation did not in itself disqualify an applicant for admission to the bar. Although the court held open the possibility of a different result where "homosexual acts" were shown, it clearly indicated that a "nexus" between that conduct and fitness for the practice of law would have to be proven, as in the Federal Civil Service decisions.

The greatest number of relevant cases to reach the state judicial systems have involved the teaching profession. All states have codes that set the standards and qualifications for teachers. Concern for the moral and professional conduct of teachers is a keystone of most state statutes. While many require the automatic revocation of the license of anyone who has been convicted of any sex offense, fitness hearings for teachers under such circumstances have been written into the laws of only a few states.

California's Education Code, for example, has been amended to permit fitness hearings for individuals convicted of sex or narcotic offences, provided: 1) they have obtained or have applied for a certificate of rehabilitation under the relevant penal code section, 2) their probation has been terminated, and 3) the information or accusation has been dismissed.[23] Since individuals convicted of misdemeanors are ineligible to apply for certificates of rehabilitation, satisfaction of the latter two requirements qualifies them for fitness hearings under the revised Code.[24] Alaska, Colorado, Connecticut, Montana, Nebraska, North Dakota, South Carolina, Texas, and Virginia have also provided for individualized consideration of fitness, despite felony or misdemeanor conviction.

The terms "immoral or unprofessional conduct" and "moral turpitude," found in typical discretionary disqualification statutes, are frequently criticized for being vague or over-broad. However, arguing that the state has a strong interest to protect the public and that all possible forms of unprofessional conduct cannot be detailed in advance, courts have traditionally refused to declare such statutes entirely void. Teachers who had been discharged under such statutes have, accordingly, won reinstatement only upon a careful weighing of the facts in individual cases and a balancing of the individual and state interests involved.

One of the first cases successfully to challenge the revocation of a teaching credential came in California. The California Supreme Court, in *Morrison* v. *State Board of Education*,[25] declined to void a statute providing for license revocation for "immoral or unprofessional conduct or moral turpitude" but construed the statute to include only conduct that indicates unfitness to teach. The court was concerned with avoiding the obvious dangers inherent in so broadly worded a statute: 1) the variance of possible interpretation depends upon time, location, context, and popular mood; 2) the lack of fair warning as to what conduct is prohibited; and 3) the danger that officials searching for signs of "immorality" might probe into the private lives of teachers. The court examined the purpose of fitness hearings and concluded that the distinction between automatic and discretionary dismissal statutes would be lost if noncriminal homosexual conduct were considered immoral per se.

The *Morrison* decision suggested that a school board should consider the following factors in determining the relationship between a teacher's conduct and fitness to teach:

the likelihood that the conduct may have adversely affected the students or fellow teachers, the degree of such adversity anticipated, the proximity or remoteness in time of the conduct, the type of teaching certification held by the teacher, the extenuating or aggravating circumstances, if any, surrounding the conduct, the praiseworthiness or blameworthiness of the motives resulting in the conduct, the likelihood of the questioned conduct, and the extent to which disciplinary action may inflict an adverse impact or chilling effect upon the constitutional rights of the teacher involved, or other teachers.[26]

Just how far the courts will carry the *Morrison* analysis is not clear. The decision itself cautions that the law does not *require* that homosexual individuals be permitted to teach in California schools. This reservation and the narrow facts of the *Morrison* case may hinder the application of its safeguards to other gay teachers. The *Morrison* analysis is significant, nevertheless, because its approach has been applied to a wide range of conduct and professions, and because recent legislative enactments are likely to increase the number of mandatory fitness hearings, placing a wider range of conduct within *Morrison's* scope. The *Morrison* analysis, however, has been applied only superficially to cases involving nonconventional sexual conduct. Since *Morrison* concerned private noncriminal acts, some courts have been eager to distinguish it on the facts despite its express purpose of retaining the distinction between automatic and discretionary disqualification statutes.

The limitation of *Morrison* to noncriminal private conduct was specifically disapproved in *Board of Education* v. *Jack M.*[27] The trial court had found that the conduct of the defendant, even though "criminal", did not evidence unfitness as a matter of law. In its unanimous decision, the Supreme Court reaffirmed the principle of appellate review that trial court findings supported by substantial evidence must be upheld, stating that "neither statute nor decisional authority has applied a rule of per se unfitness to persons who were not convicted of specified sex offenses." This decision should curb the eagerness of some school boards and courts to characterize homosexual conduct as conclusive evidence of unfitness to teach.

Even where the *Morrison* analysis has been applied, the opportunity still exists for personal prejudice to invade the process of weighing evidence. An example is *Pettit* v. *State Board of Education*,[28] where a teacher's credential revocation was upheld on the basis of her 'sexual misconduct.' The Court indicated willingness to apply what would amount to a per se rule of unfitness, by finding that the expert testimony of three school administrators was sufficient to establish unfitness, even though the testimony might be based only on personal moral views. The dissent pointed out that the "important issue of plaintiff's right to teach should not turn on the personal distaste of judges . . . "

A recurring problem in cases that do apply *Morrison* is that the courts remain free to weigh some factors heavily and to omit consideration of others entirely, as *Pettit* demonstrates. A hostile school board or trial court may disregard expert testimony supporting the teacher, and in theory, the reviewing courts may not reverse so long as there is any evidence to support the decision.

Obviously, school authorities have a legitimate concern for the safety and well-being of students. Where a teacher's conduct is directed at children, either inside or outside the classroom, it should be subject to scrutiny and sanctions. There is, however, no basis for assuming that because a teacher has been involved in heterosexual or homosexual conduct with an adult, a likelihood exists for misconduct with students. Yet many boards and courts continue to assume that homosexual orientation implies inevitable, improper, sexual conduct.

The results of litigation at the state level have not been consistent. In *Gaylord* v. *Tacoma School District*,[29] a teacher whose homosexuality was disclosed in response to questioning by his superior was dismissed soley on the basis of his homosexual status. The Washington Supreme Court affirmed, on the grounds that homosexuality was, as a matter of law, the equivalent of immorality and that the publicity created by the dismissal hearing itself adversely affected Gaylord's teaching ability. The United States Supreme Court refused review. And in *Gish* v. *Board of Education*[30] the court upheld a school board's order requiring a gay activist teacher to submit to a psychiatric examination.

III. CONCLUSION

While considerable progress has been achieved in this emerging struggle for constitutional guarantees, administrative and judicial protection for the employment opportunities of homosexual persons is generally sporadic and unreliable. Although modern research and practical experience show such opprobrium to be unwarranted and even detrimental to society, discriminatory treatment of the employment rights of gay people is still evident and still the major trend in case law.

FOOTNOTES

1. Civil Rights Act of 1964, as amended, §703, 42 U.S.C. §2000e-2 (1970).
2. *Scott v. Macy*, 349 F.2d 182 (D.C. Cir.1965), *on remand*, 402 F.2d 694 (D.C. Cir. 1968).
3. *Norton v. Macy*, 417 F.2d 1161 (D.C. Cir.1969).
4. *Schlegel v. United States*, 416 F.2d 1372 (Ct.Cl.1969).
5. *Society for Individual Rights v. Hampton*, 63 F.R.D. 399 (N.D. Cal.1973), *aff'd*, 528 F.2d 905 (9th Cir.1975).
6. United States Civil Service Commission FPM Letter 731-3, *Federal Personnel Manual System* (July 3, 1975).
7. *Singer v. Civil Service Commission*, 530 F.2d 247 (9th Cir.1976) *cert. granted*, 429 U.S. 1034 (1977).
8. *Singer v. Civil Service Commission*, United States Civil Service Commission, Federal Employee Appeals Authority, Decision No. SEO 71380002 (July 21, 1978).
9. *Saal v. Middendorf*, 427 F.Supp. 192 (N.D. Cal. 1977).
10. *See Roe v. Wade*, U.S. 113 (1973); *Griswold v. Connecticut*, 381 U.S. 479 (1965); *Cary v. Population Services International* 421 U.S. 678(1977); *Eisenstadt v. Baird*, 405 U.S. 430(1972).
11. *See* chapter by Joseph Bell, p. 97.

12. *McConnell v. Anderson*, 316 F.Supp. 809 (D.Minn. 1970).
13. Ibid., 451 F.2d 193 (8th Cir.1971), *cert. denied*, 405 U.S. 1046 (1972).
14. *Acanfora v. Board of Education*, 359 F.Supp. 843(D.Ind.1963), *aff'd*, 491 F.2d 498 (4th Cir.), *cert. denied*, 419 U.S. 835 (1974).
15. *Aumiller v. University of Delaware*, 434 F.Supp. 1273 (D.Del. 1977).
16. *Burton v. Cascade School Dist.*, 353 F.Supp. 254 (D.Oregon 1973), *aff'd*, 512 F.2d 850 (9th Cir. 1974), *cert. denied*, 423 U.S. 839 (1975).
17. *Ibid.*, 512 F.2d at 854-56 *(dissenting opinion). See* Note, "Remedial Balancing Decisions and the Rights of Homosexual Teachers: A Pyrrhic Victory," 61 Iowa L.Rev. 1080 (1976).
18. *Sail'er Inn v. Kirby*, 5 Cal. 3d 1, 485 P.2d 529, 95 Cal. Rptr. 329 (1971).
19. Executive Law, Art. 15 §290 (3) *McKinney's Consolidated Laws of New York Annotated*, p. 264.
20. *McLaughlin v. Board of Medical Examiners*, 35 Cal. App. 3d 1010, 111 Cal. Rptr. 353 (1973).
21. *In re Kimball*, 33 N.Y.2d 586, 301 N.E.2d 436, N.Y.S.2d (1973).
22. *In re Eimers*, 358 So.2d 7 (Fla.1978)___
23. Cal.Educ.Code §12910, §13175 & §13220.16 (West Supp.1977).
24. *Newland v. Board of Governors*, 19 Ca.3d 705, 566 P.2d 254, 139 Cal.Rptr. 620 (1977).
25. *Morrison v. State Board of Education*, 1 Cal.3d 214, 461 P.2d 375, 82 Cal.Rptr. 175 (1977).
26. *Ibid.* at 229, 461 P.2d at 386, 82 Cal.Rptr. at 186.
27. *Board of Education v. Jack M.*, 19 Cal.3d, 29, 566 P.2d 602, 139 Cal.Rptr. 700 (1977).
28. *Pettit v. State Board of Education*, 10 Cal.3d, 29, 513 P.2d 889, 109 Cal.Rptr. 665 (1973).
29. *Gaylord v. Tacoma School District*, 88 Wash.2d 286, 559 P.2d 1340, *cert. denied* 434 U.S. 879 (1977).
30. *Gish v. Board of Education*, 145 N.J. Super. 96, 366 A.2d 1337 (1976), *cert. denied*, 434 U.S. 869 (1977).

THE IMMIGRATION AND NATIONALITY ACT
AND THE RIGHTS OF HOMOSEXUAL ALIENS

William T. Reynolds

"Give me your tired, your poor, your huddled masses yearning to breathe free."

In 1882, four years before the Statue of Liberty was inaugurated in New York Harbor, Congress passed the "Restriction Act," which prohibited the admission of Chinese laborers to the United States.[1] Soon after, it enacted legislation providing that any Chinese resident of this country who had left temporarily, in reliance upon an exception in the Restriction Act, was forbidden to return.[2] The Supreme Court upheld the Act, holding that

[t]he power of the government to exclude foreigners from the country whenever, in its judgment, the public interests require such exclusion, has been asserted in repeated instances, and never denied by the executive or legislative departments.[3]

Thus, the High Court gave its approval to a shift in our immigration policy from one of open acceptance to the present one of severe restriction. Under this policy, Congress has virtually unlimited power to exclude any alien or group of aliens whenever it determines that such exclusion is necessary to protect "the public interests." Under the Immigration and Nationality Act of 1917, the laws are administered by a single agency, the Immigration and Naturalization Service ("I.N.S."). The Act was most recently revised in 1952, to bring the classes of excludable aliens into line with the McCarthy era's concept of "the public interests."

This article will comment critically on homosexual aliens in the 20th century and will offer a prognosis of how the Act is likely to affect them in the future. It is first necessary to distinguish among three types of situations covered by the Act: (1) exclusion, or the refusal to admit certain classes of aliens, (2) deportation of aliens who have already been admitted, and (3) naturalization of resident aliens.

William T. Reynolds is currently a student at Hastings College of the Law. He graduated with a B.A. from Haverford College in 1976.

I. EXCLUSION

Among the classes of persons excluded by the Immigration and Nationality Act are three categories that have been applied to gay persons. The first, "aliens afflicted with psychopathic personality, or a mental defect,"[4] has been interpreted to bar the entry of any person who at the time of entry acknowledges being or is found to be homosexual. The second category bars "aliens who have been convicted of a crime involving moral turpitude."[5] The phrase "moral turpitude" is not defined but the courts have construed it to mean all crimes considered repugnant to the mores of society. Typically this encompasses all sex-related crimes, whether consensual or not. The third category covers "any alien who seeks . . . to enter the United States, by fraud, or by willfully misrepresenting a material fact."[6] If a homosexual alien denies being homosexual to the I.N.S. or, having been convicted of a homosexual crime, tries to disguise the fact, that person may also be excluded.

The laws are at best arbitrarily enforced; only those homosexual persons who appear "obvious" to the I.N.S. are likely to be questioned about their sexual preferences. Furthermore, the alien has little opportunity to protest the decision. Exclusion from the United States is not considered a punitive measure, and constitutional safegards afforded citizens do not apply to the alien: An alien need receive no formal notice of charges and must bear the buden of proving the charges false at an exclusion hearing. Although technically the alien has the right to appeal through the courts, in reality this is seldom feasible. Aliens found to be excludable are sent back promptly to their points of origin and thereafter have no practical access to the American judicial system.

II. DEPORTATION

To expel an alien who has already been admitted, the government must shoulder the burden of proving that deportation is appropriate. The alien's right to judicial review *before* deportation is absolute. This structure, however, has proven to be of little assistance to the homosexual alien in the face of the authority, granted the Attorney General, to deport any alien who "at the time of entry was within one or more of the classes of aliens excludable by the law existing at the time of such entry."[7] In addition, many homosexual aliens (especially males) are deported under another section of the Act[8] if they are convicted of a "crime involving moral turpitude" within their first five years in this country.

Many gay aliens who had lost to the I.N.S. in expulsion proceedings have challenged the validity of applying such concepts as "psychopathic personality" and "crime involving moral turpitude" to homosexual persons. The courts, as a rule, have not been receptive to their arguments.

(1) "Psychopathic Personality"

The clause in the Immigration Act of 1917 that excluded "persons of constitutional psychopathic inferiority"[9] was used to bar homosexual aliens.[10] When the House of Representatives sought to revise the Act in the early 1950's, the drafters originally intended to include a provision specifically excluding "sexual perverts or homosexual persons" from entry. However, the House finally chose to rely on the somewhat ambiguous recommendation of the Public Health Services that "diagnosing" homosexuality at the borders would involve "considerable difficulty" and that "such types of pathologic behavior as homosexuality or sexual perversion" would ordinarily fall within the category of "psychopathic personality with pathologic sexuality."[11] The Act of 1952 uses only the expression "psychopathic personality."

In 1962, a Swiss citizen living in California challenged a deportation order on the ground that "the statute failed to advise him that homosexual practices conclusively evidence a 'psychopathic personality'."[12] The Ninth Circuit Court of Appeals agreed with him and declared that section of the Act void for vagueness. Eventually, by reversing the circuit court's decision (albeit on other grounds), the Supreme Court deprived it of precedential value.

The Act's potential for vagueness was eliminated in 1965, when Congress amended it to include "sexual deviation" as a ground for exclusion.[13] This amendment applies only to aliens admitted after its enactment; thus, in 1966, the Ninth Circuit again reversed an order for deportation of a gay alien who had been admitted prior to the amendment.[14] But in 1965, the Second Circuit reached a different conclusion in *Boutilier v. I.N.S.*,[15] and the Supreme Court granted review.

Boutilier was a Canadian national who had lived in New York as a permanent resident since 1955. He applied for citizenship in 1963 and confessed that he had been arrested in 1959 on a sodomy charge. The charge had been reduced to simple assault and later dismissed by default. When the I.N.S. requested a full history of his "sexual deviate behavior," Boutilier admitted that prior to entry he had had homosexual relations on an average of three or four times a year, as well as heterosexual relations on a few occasions. The I.N.S. then obtained a certificate from the Public Health Service stating that Boutilier "was afflicted with a Class A condition, namely, psychopathic personality." Deportation proceedings were instituted, and the order followed.

In his appeal, Boutilier argued that the term "psychopathic personality" was vague when used as a legal term. He attempted to show that it was a medical term and that medical testimony should, therefore, be admissible in his defense.[16] The wording of the revised Act was, after all, patterned on the recommendation of the Public Health Service.

The Supreme Court (with Justices Douglas, Fortas, and Brennan dissenting) declared Boutilier's contentions to be without merit. The Court held that the term "psychopathic personality" was one of legal art; it did not matter whether different psychiatrists might disagree on its meaning or application to homosexuality. "The test here is what Congress intended," the Court reasoned, and the "legislative history of the Act indicated beyond a shadow of a doubt that the Congress intended the phrase 'psychopathic personality' to include homosexuals such as petitioner."[17]

(2) "Crimes Involving Moral Turpitude"

"Moral turpitude" is another term of legal art. It has never been defined precisely but was designed to encompass all crimes that are considered abominable by society at any given time. The term has withstood a test of constitutionality,[18] and has been held sufficiently broad to include such crimes as solicitation, the commission "by any male person of any acts of gross indecency with another male person" in public or private, and indecent assault.[19]

Any person who has been convicted of such a crime before entry to the United States is subject to deportation on the grounds of having belonged to an excludable class at the time of entry. In addition, an alien may be deported if convicted of such a crime within five years after entry and sentenced to prison for a year or more, or if convicted of two such crimes at any time after entry.

In *Babouris* v. *Esperdy*,[20] a Greek citizen who had lived in the United States since 1920 appealed a deportation order on the ground that loitering and soliciting men "for the purpose of committing a crime against nature or other lewdness"[21] (of which he had been twice convicted) was considered an "offense", rather than a crime or misdemeanor, under New York law. The court held "that the peculiar New York definition of the word 'crime' " could not control the interpretation of the Immigration Act, since the same "offense" is considered a crime in most other states. The court gave no indication as to how this argument would be applied to an alien convicted of a crime (such as consensual sodomy) in one state when the same act would not be considered criminal in many other states.

It is interesting to compare this case with *Velez-Lozano* v. *I.N.S.*,[22] which involved a male alien who had been convicted of consensual sodomy with a woman. Although the court upheld the deportation order, it expressed reluctance at having to reach this decision. If permitted, the court would have given effect to the sentencing judge's recommendation against deportation:

Deportation here would be harsh and unjustifiable. While the Service has the legal *power and authority this Court hopes that they take a moment to examine the* equities *of this case before proceeding further.*[23]

The courts have expressed no such leniency or compassion in cases involving homosexual persons, even where (as with Babouris) no sexual act — legal or illegal — was proven.

(3) Misrepresentation

The courts have held that the Fifth Amendment guarantee of protection from self-incrimination is inapplicable to deportation proceedings, on the ground that deportation, while a more drastic measure than exclusion, is not considered criminal punishment. Thus, a gay alien may be deported for admitting a sexual preference, for admitting conviction of a crime, or for not admitting either.

In *United States* v. *Flores-Rodriguez,*[24] a Cuban national who visited the United States in 1950 was arrested in a New York public toilet. In 1952 he returned to America and applied for permanent residence, stating that he had not been arrested, indicted, or convicted of any offense. When he was arrested for the same offense in 1954, he was charged with perjury and ordered deported. On appeal, the court upheld both the perjury conviction and the deportation order, finding that his misrepresentation was tantamount to perjury in and of itself, and also prevented an investigation of other possible grounds for excluding him. As an example, the court cited the section of the Act excluding persons "afflicted with . . . a mental defect,"[25] language that the court felt "was designed to exclude homosexuals with exhibitionist tendencies and other groups with lewd proclivities similarly repugnant to the mores of our society."[26]

III. NATURALIZATION

If an alien has been legally admitted to the U.S. and has lived here for a period of at least five years, he or she is eligible to file a petition for naturalization. To be granted citizenship, the alien must have been "a person of good moral character"[27] during the five-year period preceding the petition. A finding of good moral character would be denied where the petitioner has been convicted of a crime involving moral turpitude during that period.[28]

In re Schmidt involved a citizen of Denmark, legally admitted to the United States in 1948, who filed a petition for naturalization in 1962. Her testimony revealed that she had engaged in sexual activites with six women in this country since her arrival. After a deportation proceeding was terminated for lack of evidence that she was a "sexual deviate" at the time of entry, her naturalization petition was denied for lack of good moral character. She appealed to a New York court, arguing that the I.N.S. had failed to disclose any criminal convictions, dismissals from employment for sexual deviation, or anything else of a derogatory nature.

The court found this testimony irrelevant. The tests for determining "good moral character," it said, are "the ethical standards current at the time . . . [,] the response that the 'ordinary' man or woman would make." The court reasoned that Schmidt's petition should be dismissed, since "few behavioral deviations are more offensive to American mores than is homosexuality . . . "[29]

More recently, however, courts applying this standard have begun to recognize that the "ethical standards" of America today are somewhat more relaxed with regard to homosexuality. In *Kovacs* v. *United States*,[30] a Hungarian who filed for naturalization in 1968 made the mistake of denying his homosexuality in the face of evidence produced by the I.N.S. that showed he had, in a criminal trial, admitted to participating in many homosexual acts, "including about fifty acts of fellatio per year since 1959." On appeal, the court upheld the dismissal of his petition, but made it clear that

[p]etitioner is not being denied naturalization for his sexual activities—but rather for his lack of candor under oath . . . Had Kovacs testified truthfully about his past, the petition might well have been granted.[31]

Finally, in *In re Brodie*,[32] a federal district court in Oregon granted a petition for naturalization despite the fact that the alien was known to be homosexual. The court noted that Brodie was a veteran of the U.S. Army, had never been sexually involved with minors, had never given or taken money for sex, and had no criminal record nor any history of sexual activities in any public places. The district judge concluded that

I have little difficulty finding that Brodie's conduct is acceptable by the ethical standards of the year 1975 . . . I am not required to find that (it) conforms to the preferences of the majority. Plainly it does not. I need only find that it does not so offend that the "ordinary" person . . . would think it immoral.[33]

This opinion is clearly an important step toward eventual legitimization of homosexuality. A problem remains, however, with the standard used to determine "good moral character." In deciding the "ethical standards of the year 1975" of Brodies's community (Portland, Oregon), the court cited the repeal of the Oregon sodomy statute in 1971; the resolution banning discrimination in employment on the basis of sexual preference, which was passed by the Portland City Council in 1974; and the removal of homosexuality from the American Psychiatric Association's list of mental illnesses. What would be the result if Brodie lived in nearby Eugene and his case were heard today? Or if the A.P.A. were to decide to re-instate homosexuality as a disease? In other words, should the standard of "good moral character" be subject to the whims of a certain community, or of American society in general?

At least one court has held that it should not. *In re Labady*[34] concerned a Cuban refugee who had come to the United States in 1960, at age 14. Labady admitted his homosexuality upon entry, but the I.N.S. chose to overlook this, possibly because of his age or refugee status. When he filed his petition for naturalization in 1969, however, it was denied on the basis of his sexual preference. Labady appealed to the New York federal district court. He offered evidence that all of his homosexual activities had been in private with consenting adults; that he had never been arrested; that he did not drink, frequent bars, or use narcotics; that he had never "been in trouble" and was "highly regarded at his place of employment."

The court granted Labady's petition, holding that his sexual life was not in itself indicative of bad moral character. This holding was based not on the moral standards of the "ordinary" person, but rather on the distinction between public and private sexual activity:

We believe that the most important factor to be considered is whether the challenged conduct is public or private in nature . . . If . . . it is entirely private, the likelihood of harm to others is minimal and any effort to regulate or penalize the conduct may lead to an unjustified invasion of the individual's constitutional rights . . . In short, private conduct which is not harmful to others, even though it may violate the personal moral code of most of us, does not violate public morality . . .[35]

The court goes on to discuss "the relative complacency" with which the public tends to view homosexuality these days, but it is clear that this is only a secondary consideration. The main point is that a person's private sexual life has no bearing upon the question of moral character.

The Immigration and Naturalization Service, in light of the above holdings, has recently announced a change in its policy of denying citizenship to homosexual aliens. In an internal opinion published in 1977, the Service takes the position that, "(t)he fact that a petitioner (for naturalization) is or has been practicing private homosexual acts with consenting adults during the relevant statutory period is not, in itself, a sufficient basis for a finding that he or she lacks the necessary good moral character where the homosexual conduct is not a criminal offense under the law of the jurisdiction."[36]

However, the interpretation goes on to say that such a finding could be reached if other factors were present. These include not only conviction of a crime involving homosexuality, homosexual acts involving minors, payment, threat or fraud, and public solicitations, but also the *admission* of engaging in homosexual acts in any jurisdiction in which such acts remain criminal.

A recent immigration decision consistent with this policy is *Petition of Longstaff*,[37] in which a naturalization examiner analyzed the *Labady, Brodie,* and *Kovacs* decisions and concluded that "being a homosexual in and of itself does not preclude a petitioner from showing good moral character." The petitioner in *Longstaff* had admitted to having consensual homosexual relations, which were criminal in the state of his residence; but the examiner noted that factors such as minors, threats, fraud, prostitution, or public solicitation were not involved. The examiner, therefore, concluded that good moral character had been shown and recommended naturalization.

IV. CONCLUSION

While the prospects for naturalization of openly gay aliens have improved in recent years, the present statutory and administrative framework cotinues to be riddled with exceptions and outdated standards. A much more significant development has occurred recently in the area of exclusion and deportation. Though the Supreme Court has not reexamined the position it took in the *Boutilier* case, the Public Health Service has announced a policy change whereby homosexual persons will no longer be classified as "sexual deviants" or "psychopathic personalities" upon entry.[38]

This action should have the effect of removing those categories from the realm of legal terminology and restoring to them their original status as medical terms, if the policy is not challenged in the courts or altered by the Congress. If it is, the judiciary will be forced to decide between the policy of *Boutilier* and the medical judgment of the Public Health Service.

FOOTNOTES

1. Act of 1882, 22 Stat. 58, c. 126, *as amended,* July 5, 1884, 23 Stat. 115, c. 220.
2. Act of 1888, 25 Stat. 504, c. 1064.
3. *The Chinese Exclusion Case*, 130 U.S. 581 (1889).
4. 8 U.S.C. § 1182 (a)(4).
5. 8 U.S.C. § 1182 (a)(9).
6. 8 U.S.C. § 1182 (a)(19).
7. 8 U.S.C. § 1251 (a)(1).
8. 8 U.S.C. § 1251 (a)(4).
9. 8 U.S.C. § 136 (a)(1946).
10. *In re Steele*, 12 I. & N. Dec. 302 (BIA, 1967).
11. H. R. Rep. No. 1365, 82d Cong., 2d Sess., 1952 *U.S. Code Cong. & Admin. News* 1701.

12. *Fleuti* v. *Rosenberg*, 302 F.2d 652 (9th Cir. 1962), *rev'd on other grounds*, 374 U.S. 449 (1963).
13. 8 U.S.C. § 1182 (a) (4), *as amended*, 1965.
14. *Lavoie* v. *I.N.S.*, 360 F.2d 27 (9th Cir. 1966), *Vacated in light of Boutilier v. I.N.S.*, 387 U.S. 572, *amended*, 389 U.S. 908 (1967).
15. *Boutilier* v. *I.N.S.*, 363 F.2d 488 (2d Cir. 1965).
16. *Boutilier* v. *I.N.S.*, 387 U.S. 188 (1967).
17. *Ibid.*
18. *Jordan* v. *De George*, 341 U.S. 223 (1951).
19. *In re Matter of H -*, I. & N. Dec. 359 (BIA, 1957).
20. *Babouris* v. *Esperdy*, 296 F. 2d 621 (2d Cir. 1959).
21. N.Y. Penal Law § 722 (8).
22. *Velez-Lozano* v. *I.N.S.*, 463 F.2d 1305 (D.C. Cir. 1972).
23. *Ibid.*
24. *U.S.* v. *Flores-Rodriguez*, 237 F.2d 405 (2d Cir. 1956).
25. 8 U.S.C. § 1182 (a) (4).
26. *U.S.* v. *Flores-Rodriguez, supra.*
27. 8 U.S.C. § 1427 (a) (3).
28. 8 U.S.C. § 1101 (f) (3).
29. *In re schmidt*, 289 N.Y.Supp.2d 89 (Sup.Ct. Duchess Co. 1968).
30. *Kovacs* v. *U.S.*, 476 F.2d 843 (2d Cir. 1973).
31. *Ibid.*
32. *In re Brodie*, 394 F. Supp. 1208 (D. Ore. 1975).
33. *Ibid.*
34. *In re Labady*, 326 F.Supp. 924 (S.D.N.Y. 1971).
35. *Ibid.*
36. I.N.S. Interpretations § 316.1 (f) (7), at 5246. 10-5246.11 (June 22, 1977) (unpublished; copy on file at Gay Rights Advocates, San Francisco).
37. *Petition of Longstaff*, A14-533-708 (N.D. Tex., Apr. 14, 1978).
38. "It's Time" (Newsletter of the National Gay Task Force), vol. 5, no. 5 (May 1978).

SOCIAL ATTITUDES, LEGAL STANDARDS AND PERSONAL TRAUMA IN CHILD CUSTODY CASES

Donna Hitchens, J.D.

I. INTRODUCTION

To most people, the idea of a person being both homosexual and a parent is inherently inconsistent. In fact there are many homosexual parents,[1] but until recently there were almost no reported judicial decisions dealing with their rights as fathers and mothers. Two reasons explain why: First, most homosexual parents have worked very hard to conceal their sexual orientation from their children, their families, and their ex-spouses; second, often if someone discovered or suspected that a parent was homosexual the parent gave up custody or visitation "voluntarily" rather than face a long, expensive, and public court case. It has generally been assumed not only that the homosexual parent would eventually lose the case, but also that the inevitable publicity would jeopardize other aspects of the parent's life, such as their employment and living situations.

Since the late 1960's, more and more gay parents have been unwilling to keep their sexual preference secret and have refused to concede their parental rights. For whatever reason, be it the emergence of support and pride from the women's and gay rights movements, or some other cause, fewer parents are permitting society to force them to choose between their sexual preference and the custody of their children.

It should be noted that the majority of custody cases reported concern lesbian mothers. Most of the cases involving gay fathers deal with the right to visit with their children and the conditions under which that right may be exercised. As this article treats the problems of custody, the discussion will focus primarily on lesbians. It is fair to assume that the issues are the same for gay fathers seeking custody, with the additional burden of confronting the sexist belief that children should always be cared for by their mothers.

Donna Hitchens is Directing Attorney of the Lesbian Rights Project and of the Vocational Education Project, Equal Rights Advocates, Inc., both of San Francisco. She serves on the board of directors for the Northern California American Civil Liberties Union and for Gay Rights Advocates. She received her J.D. from the University of California, Berkeley.

II. THE LEGAL PREDICAMENT OF GAY FATHERS AND LESBIAN MOTHERS

Before discussing the specifics of what happens to gay fathers and lesbian mothers once engaged in a contest for custody, it is important to understand the setting in which these parents find themselves. The American legal system has not accepted the notion that a good parent may also be homosexual. The system is dominated by judges, lawyers, and legislators — most of whom are white, male, heterosexual, and middle class, who subscribe to the popular social values. The obvious result is that society's assumptions and prejudices regarding both homosexuality and the proper way to raise children are reflected in the laws and court decisions.

Several recurring themes emerge in judicial decisions involving a homosexual parent. First, there is the concern that being raised in a gay household will stigmatize a child and create conflicts between the child and the child's peer group. Even in cases in which a child has not experienced problems, judges, probation officers, and psychiatrists have assumed that trouble will develop in the future and, therefore, that the child would be better off living in a heterosexual home. For example, in a 1978 California case a clinical psychologist testified that it would be detrimental to the children to allow them to continue living with their lesbian mother because there was a "definite possibility" of peer ridicule in the future. On cross-examination by the mother's attorney, the psychologist testified as follows:

Psychologist: They are really amazing little girls. They're very bright ...
Attorney: When you suggest that a change of custody would be appropriate, that's because of your fears for the future, is that it?
Pshychologist: That's correct.
Attorney: Not because of anything that you presently see wrong with the children?
Psychologist: No, that's right. That's right.[2]

Second, there continues to be a substantial fear, despite the absence of any supporting evidence, that children raised in a gay home will grow up to be homosexual or develop "improper" sex-role behavior. The clinical psychologist in the California case mentioned above also testified that were they to continue living with their mother and her lover, the children might

pick up mannerisms, the behavior, and the way of speaking and talking, and gait, and other things that are likely to be decisive in which way these girls will go with their sexual identification at this particular time and over the next few years.[3]

On cross-examination, the psychologist could not give any examples of horrid gait, speech, or mannerisms which the children might imitate from their mother.

Third, it is widely presumed that, given a choice between a heterosexual and homosexual home environment, the heterosexual home is unquestionably better for a child. Once again, no specific reason is provided to support the presumption — it is a given. Occasionally, courts take the position that a heterosexual home provides better role-modeling and a better moral environment than does a lesbian home. The more common approach is simply to state, as did one Court of Appeal:

In exercising a choice between homosexual and heterosexual households for purposes of child custody a trial court could conclude that permanent residence in a homosexual household would be detrimental to the children and contrary to their best interests.[4]

Fourth, although it is the general practice of our legal system to treat the parent-child relationship with respect and deference, the courts have the duty to intervene for the protection of the child. Unfortunately, in applying this principle a court may conclude that the child's welfare requires removal from the custody of a homosexual parent.

The result is that lesbian mothers and gay fathers live with a constant threat of losing their parental rights. Almost anyone can challenge an individual's custody of their children. Although the most common occasion for dispute is between parents during the dissolution of a marriage, the right to custody may also be challenged by other relatives or by government authorities. Since the legal system responds somewhat differently to child custody disputes depending on the parties involved, the various challenges will be discussed separately.[5]

A. Disputes Between Parents

At the time of a divorce, legal provision must be made for the custody of any minor children. If the parents agree who will be the custodial parent and what visitation rights the other parent will have, the process is relatively simple. If, however, the parents cannot agree, a judge must determine where the children will live and what rights each parent will have.

In disputes between two parents, both are now presumed in most states to have an equal right to custody of the children. In deciding between the parents, the judge is given an enormous amount of discretion and is rarely reversed on appeal. Generally, the sole principle guiding the judge is to decide in accordance with the "best interest of the child". The "best interest" standard has no legal definition — there are no objective guidelines to assist in deciding what constitutes "best interest". Common considerations in these cases include: (1) with whom the child has been living since the parents separated, (2) the home environments of both parents, (3) the financial abilities of both parents, and (4) whether one parent is better able to provide for the health or special needs of a child. The judge may also hear evidence on any other issues considered relevant, including the sexual behavior of the parents.

The homosexuality of a parent is a powerful weapon that can be used to prevent or limit their custodial or visitation rights. Typically, once it has been brought to the court's attention that the father is gay or the mother lesbian, almost all other evidence becomes secondary. The trial thereafter focuses almost exclusively on the issue of homosexuality, with the homosexual parent trying to convince the judge that there will be no detrimental effect on the child and with the other parent arguing that the child will surely be stigmatized, traumatized, or confused sexually if allowed to live in a homosexual environment

Although there have been a few cases in which appellate courts have held that a mother's lesbianism does not, in itself, render her an unfit parent, these cases have not had a great impact on child custody litigation. This is because in applying the "best interest" standard it is not necessary for one parent to be found unfit. In determining which of the two parents should have custody, a judge can simply decide that it is in the child's best interest to be with the heterosexual parent. There is no requirement that a judge articulate a specific connection (or "nexus") between the mother's lesbianism and its effects on her children before denying her custody on the basis of her sexual orientation.

The outcome of a lesbian mother's custody case is often unpredictable — some lesbians have been successful in their legal battles to retain the children, while others have lost custody of their children after years of being the primary parent. Even when a lesbian mother is granted custody of her children, it may be on the condition that she agree not to live with her lover and not to participate in certain public political or social events.

The extreme fear and prejudice triggered by the notion of a homosexual parent is evident in a number of cases involving the right of noncustodial fathers and mothers to visit their children. It is not uncommon to find that the right to visitation is predicated upon the total absence of a lover — or any homosexual friend — during the visit or upon the presence of a heterosexual adult while the parent is visiting with the children.

B. *Custody Disputes with Relatives*

An unusually high number of lesbian mother cases involve legal disputes between the mother and another relative, often a grandparent. Whereas a mother and father may be equally entitled to the custody of their children, a parent is generally considered to have a greater right to custody than does a nonparent relative. In some states, before a child can be taken from a parent and placed in the custody of a nonparent, the judge must determine that it would be detrimental to the child to continue living with the natural parent or that the parent is unfit. Legally, the detrimental determination places a greater burden of proof on those challenging the parent's right to custody than does the "best interest of the child" standard.

However, a review of the cases in which the dispute is between a lesbian mother and another relative reveals that the lesbian mother does not benefit greatly from the legal preference for the natural parent. The courts retain the discretion to *presume* that it would be detrimental to the children to allow them to live with a lesbian mother and judges are free to apply their own value judgments in determining what is detrimental. There is no requirement that the court demonstrate a connection between the mother's lesbianism and the presumed detrimental impact it would have on her children.

C. *State Intervention into the Parent-Child Relationship*

Action by government authorities to remove a child from the custody of its parents is generally recognized as a very serious matter and the avenue of last resort. It is action to be taken only when some behavior, such as neglect or abuse by the parent, severely harms a child. Sometimes situations arise where a parent is arrested or hospitalized and the state authorities, usually child protective services, enter to ensure that the children receive proper care during the period of the parent's absence from home. If, in the course of this process, a mother's lesbianism is discovered, there may be an attempt to place the children in foster care.

Despite the gravity of such intervention, there have been cases in which children were removed from the home and placed in foster care merely because the court believed that exposure of the children to a continuing lesbian relationship involved "the necessary likelihood of serious adjustment problems."[6]

III. DECISIONS, CHOICES, AND PERSONAL TRAUMA

Regardless of whether a parent has ever been involved in a court challenge, the threat of losing the custody of one's children — or being forced to choose between one's lover and a child — is an everyday reality for homosexual fathers and mothers. Gay parents are aware that their sexual orientation can all too easily be used against them by ex-spouses, family, or state authorities. Decisions about how to live, with whom to live, how to raise children, whether to "come out," and whether to become involved in political activities, all have potentially severe legal consequences bearing on the right to remain a parent.

Once a homosexual parent becomes involved in a child custody contest, every facet of their life is open to the court's scrutiny. It is common for the judge or for the other parent's attorney to ask questions regarding the homosexual parent's sexual partners, about the amount of affection the parent shows to a lover while the children are present, whether the parent is active in gay rights organizations, whether the parent associates with other "known homosexuals," and whether the children play with the toys "appropriate" to their biological sex. In one case, the judge actually asked the lesbian mother:

Ma'am, will you explain to the Court exactly what occurs — we talk here generally of a homosexual act. Just what does this entail? What do you do?[7]

Judges and lawyers will often insinuate or directly accuse homosexual parents of molesting their own children, of not caring about them, or of having sexual relations in front of their children. The affront to a homosexual parent's dignity is constant throughout a court proceeding. Almost all of the individual's strength and energy is consumed in dealing with the legal system, leaving the parent to feel they have little remaining to offer a lover, children, or friends.

Perhaps the most devastating blow comes when a lesbian mother is told she may have custody of the children only if she does not live with her lover. Except in the most extreme cases of physical abuse, no court would tell a heterosexual person to choose between a spouse and children. But it is common in lesbian mother cases for the children and the mother to be denied the right to live as members of a family headed by two unmarried women.

Even in situations in which gay parents have been granted visitation or custody rights, the ordeal is not over. Child custody orders are subject to modification, and the possibility remains that a case may be re-opened at any time. If the custody or visitation order is accompanied by any conditions, such as the presence of another adult during visitation, the homosexual parent must be unswervingly diligent in abiding by those conditions.

It is crucial that the personal trauma involved in litigating a child custody case be understood not only by gay parents, but also by their lovers, lawyers, counselors, friends, and community supporters. This understanding is critical in developing a sound strategy and network of support for those who are willing to fight for their rights both to be parents and to love whom and how they choose.

IV. CONCLUSION

Gay parents shoulder a staggering burden of present and potential troubles. The problems, however, are not insurmountable. It is important to note that lesbian mother custody cases and gay father visitation cases are increasingly successful in the courts. The main hurdle continues to be the lack of objective legal standards that could make the outcome of these cases predictable and sensible. That can be accomplished only by concentrated efforts in the following areas: (1) education of lawyers and judges concerning the realities of homosexuality, (2) sophisticated social science research directed at combating the assumptions and fears to which homosexual parents are currently subjected, and (3) development of interdisciplinary support systems to assist homosexual parents who are involved in court proceedings related to their parental rights. Because of the impact of, and interaction between, social attitudes, legal standards, and personal trauma in child custody cases, it is clear that the availability of legal representation is not, in itself, sufficient to guarantee to homosexual persons their right to be parents.

FOOTNOTES

1. It has been estimated that as many as 20% of all lesbians are mothers. See Hunter & Polikoff, *Custody Rights of Lesbian Mothers: Legal Theory and Litigation Strategy*, 25 Buffalo L. Rev. 691, fn. 1 (1976).
2. *Smith v. Smith*, Civ. No. 125497 (Superior Court of California, County of Stanislaus), (1978), Reporter's Transcript, p. 38.
3. *Id.*, p. 41.
4. *Chaffin v. Frye*, 45 Cal. App. 3d 39, 47, 119 Cal. Rptr. 22, 26 (1975).
5. For a more complete discussion of lesbian and gay parent cases, the legal standards applied by the courts, and references to social science data, see Hunter & Polikoff, *op. cit.*; Basile, *Lesbian Mother I*, 2 Women's Rights L. Rptr. 3 (1974); and Note, *The Avowed Lesbian Mother and Her Right to Child Custody: A Constitutional Challenge That Can No Longer Be Denied*, 12 San Diego L. Rev. 799 (1975).
6. *In the Matter of Tammy F.*, 1 Civ. No. 32648 (Cal. 1st App. Dist. Div. 2, 1973).
7. *Nadler v. Nadler*, Civ. No. 177331, (Superior Court of California, County of Sacramento), (1967), Reporter's Transcript, p. 20.

PUBLIC MANIFESTATIONS OF PERSONAL MORALITY: LIMITATIONS ON THE USE OF SOLICITATION STATUTES TO CONTROL HOMOSEXUAL CRUISING

Joseph J. Bell, J.D.

I. INTRODUCTION

A man is in a bar, another sits next to him, smiles. "Hi." "Hi." Knees touch. "Wanna get together?" "Okay." Outside, the first man is confronted by another man; both the man who invited him and the one approaching are cops. "You're under arrest!"—and the nightmare begins. Handcuffs. You see the despising face that smiled and encouraged earlier. Jail doors lock. Found guilty of lewd conduct, you'll have to register as a sex offender—all because you accepted an invitation to sex![1]

Romantic love between men has been the subject of comment and controversy since the earliest recorded times. D. J. West notes that one of the oldest poems in existence, the *Epic of Gilgamesh*, composed in 2000 B.C. or earlier, tells a story of love between two male warriors.[2] The theme of male love inspiring heroism is recurrent in the epics and legends of classical Greece. Nevertheless, homosexuality, though nearly universal in human society, has often met with popular mockery and constraint.[3]

American society and its long history of puritanism have brought homophobia "to an apex that has no parallel in modern civilized society."[4] As the celebrated Kinsey study noted, there are few cultures in the world so disturbed by male homosexuality as is the United States.[5]

In recent decades the manner in which Western societies, and the United States in particular, deal with this contradiction between individual behavior and societal attitudes has shifted markedly. The past ten years have witnessed increased openness by homosexual men and women, as well as widespread public discussion of this formerly taboo subject in

Mr. Bell received his B.A., 1969, University of Nevada, Reno, Nevada; and J.D. 1979, New College of California School of Law, San Francisco, California; he is currently Law Clerk, San Francisco Neighborhood Legal Assistance Foundation, San Francisco, California.

the popular and professional media. As recently as 1948, the mere intimation that more than a third of the total American male population had experienced homosexual activity[6] caused considerable controversy. Thereafter, the focus of concern shifted to the legitimacy of homosexuality as an alternative form of sexual relationship. Following a period of increased political and social activism by gay people in late 1973, the American Psychiatric Association removed homosexuality from its list of mental disorders,[7] but not without steadfast opposition on the part of many psychiatrists. There remains in American culture a strong resistance to legitimizing any form of homosexual behavior.[8] This hostility is rooted primarily in religious concepts that advocate lifelong monogamy and the production of children. Though these concepts have been challenged by easier access to contraceptives and divorce, fear and hatred of homosexuality continue to fuel controversies, such as whether homosexual teachers are, per se, unfit to teach.

This chapter discusses the centrality of "cruising" to the male homosexual milieu and the legal relationship of cruising to the predominantly heterosexual mores of American society. Of primary interest is the use of criminal sanctions to prohibit "solicitation" of "lewd and lascivious" acts. The language and history of California's solicitation laws are discussed as examples of imprecise expressions of legislative intent arguably violating the rights of free speech, privacy, and due process of law. Finally, the social implications of maintaining such a system of behavioral control are explored, and alternatives presently before the courts and legislature in California are discussed. Since women are apparently not involved in cruising to any substantial degree,[9] they are not generally prosecuted for noncommercial solicitation. The discussion will focus, then, on male homosexual adults in California.

II. HOMOSEXUAL CRUISING

The recent study by the Kinsey Institute of homosexual persons in the San Francisco area defines "cruising" as a "purposive search for a sexual partner."[10] The Kinsey study, which involved a sample of nearly a thousand homosexual men and women, concluded that

public cruising is infrequent among lesbians and that, among homosexual men who cruise in public places, most conduct their sexual activity in the privacy of their homes.[11]

Because cruising usually results in private encounters of at least several hours' duration, the researchers concluded that such contacts "must often involve friendly, non-sexual kinds of interaction."[12] Certainly this belies the traditional image of offensive, obvious, sexual advances followed by public sexual acts.

Cruising may be condemned as depravity or it may be elevated to the status of a political principle, as by John Rechy in *The Sexual Outlaw*. Rechy, who regards cruising as a political confrontation, described the promiscuous homosexual male as a sexual revolutionary who constantly battles

repressive laws, repressive "morality." Parks, alleys, subway tunnels, garages, streets—these are the battlefields.

To the sexhunt he brings a sense of choreography, ritual and mystery—sexcruising with an electrified instinct that sends and receives messages of orgy at any moment, any place.[13]

This picture is compatible with the stereotyped sexual profligacy of the homosexual male. The most recent survey of a large homosexual population, however, reveals that cruising is neither universal nor necessarily aggressive. In this survey almost half the respondents indicated that it was their prospective partner, rather than themselves, who made the first approach. Nor is cruising uniformly voracious: age and other demographic factors apparently affect the nature and frequency of cruising. Finally, few respondents cruised in public restrooms or movie theaters, or in bars where there was danger of arrest or physical assault.[14]

Perhaps a description of cruising as "unfocused interaction"[15] would be more generally applicable. Goffman described such interaction as consisting of those interpersonal communications that result

solely by virtue of persons being in one another's presence, as when two strangers across the room from each other check up on each other's clothing, posture and general manner, while each modifies his own demeanor because he himself is under observation.[16]

This description appears to fit precisely the interrelations of homosexual men cruising in a gay bar.

The conclusion to be drawn from the variety of definitions of "cruising" is that the term covers an extremely broad area of behavior, ranging from the exchange of casual glances to physical contact, and involving speech and behavior to be found in many nonsexual forms of human interaction as well. Furthermore, as the San Francisco study documented, a wide variety of homosexual relationships exists. Some men frequently exchange affection in abbreviated encounters that cannot be labeled promiscuous. Others are involved in lengthy and even lifetime relationships.

The social and psychological catalysts for cruising have not been studied adequately. The literature has tended toward "ethnographic" descriptions of certain homosexual locales or toward psychiatric explanations based on disease, immorality, or heterosexual inadequacy. A preference for promiscuous sexuality seems to derive from biological factors, social advantages, and psychological motivations. Tripp argues that homosexual promiscuity rests, in part, on a combination of ready opportunity and

biological traditions—a high sex-drive, an easily triggered responsiveness, and, perhaps, a kind of species history of the sexual chase.[17]

In addition to feelings of acceptance or appreciation, other emotions that surpass those attached to "pure sex" may be involved. Affection may be promiscuity's motivating force or its salient, even if unexpected, result.[18] Alternatively, affection may be totally absent, due to barriers deliberately maintained by the participants. Pejorative implications need not be drawn here, since sexual contact can be "personally meaningful without being interpersonally so."[19] Very powerful motives for promiscuity may be fantasy, intrigue, or simple novelty. The social status of one who "plays the field" is an additional motivating reward to the ego.

Hoffman, however, theorized that social repression of homosexual males results in promiscuous sexuality:

[T]he instability of relationships which is frequently used as grounds for condemnation of homosexuals is, in fact, the very product of this condemnation . . . (;) it is the social prohibitions they suffer which largely prevent them from being involved in relationships.[20]

Rechy would agree:

For centuries homosexuals . . . have been prosecuted and persecuted. The law tells us we're criminals and so we've become defiant outlaws . . . The impermanency you've pushed on us, we've converted from an aimless hell into, at best, a joyous promiscuity to confront you and your permanence.[21]

Alternatively, the authors of the recent San Francisco study found that

[h]omosexuals' sexual activity . . . commonly begins with highly cautious pursuits in places not normally frequented by heterosexuals or in more public surroundings where heterosexuals are not aware of what is taking place.[22]

More than ten years ago the noted *U. C. L. A. Law Review* study[23] concluded that most homosexual males who are cruising for partners do not brazenly pursue the first opportunity but seek some responsiveness before initiating an unequivocal approach. While homosexual cruising is experienced by the participants as being ubiquitous and intense, it is often so circumspect as to go unrecognized by others until public physical contact results.

Many long-term relationships start with casual cruising and contact. Tripp states that more than half the ongoing relationships examined in the course of his study began as brief encounters.[24] This is not surprising if we accept Hoffman's reasoning that much homosexual promiscuity can be explained by the fact that homosexual men and women cannot

meet as homosexuals in the kinds of social settings in which heterosexuals can (e.g., at school, at work) where the emphasis on finding sexual partners is not the controlling force behind all the social interaction which transpires.[25]

The prospect of immediate sexual satisfaction combines with nonsexual social patterns to give cruising a position in the gay social milieu comparable to that of heterosexual courtship in a "singles" bar.

III. CRIMINALIZATION OF HOMOSEXUAL INTERACTION

A. Statutory Background

Sexual solicitation laws have been interpreted to apply to all of the speech and behavior characterized as "cruising" above. "Solicitation" is defined legally as "any action which the relation of the parties justifies in construing into a serious request,"[26] including, therefore, both speech and conduct resulting in a request.

Solicitation is one of the so-called "inchoate," or unfinished, crimes. It has an uncertain common law history and is the explicit subject of statutes in only a minority of jurisdictions.[27] The common law crime of solicitation is limited to those instances in which the crime solicited is either a felony or some serious breach of the peace or public welfare. Most state laws rely on the common law, specifically criminalizing only those forms of solicitation, such as offering bribes or inciting riots, that in themselves constitute particularly serious threats to the social order.[28]

The justifications for criminalization are : (1) that it provides a basis for timely law enforcement intervention to prevent the intended crime, (2) that it permits the criminal justice system to deal with individuals who have indicated their "dangerousness," and (3) that it avoids inequality of treatment based on the fortuitous response of the person solicited.[29] It is questionable whether these purposes are in fact served by disorderly conduct statutes that criminalize solicitations for conduct denominated "lewd," "dissolute," or "lascivious."

These statues originated in the English Act of 1898, which sought to punish any "male person who in any public place persistently solicits or importunes for immoral purposes." It is important to note that the statutory language of the 1898 Act required *persistence* and an "immoral" purpose, usually prostitution. Those limitations did not, however, prevent the law from becoming a tool for social control of homosexuality in general.[30]

Solicitation statutes have served to criminalize homosexual behavior that, among heterosexual people, would not be punishable. The courts have generally been reluctant to impose even civil sanctions on heterosexual importuning:

Even the dire affront of inviting an unwilling woman to illicit intercourse has been held by most courts to be no such outrage as to lead to liability, —the view being, apparently in Judge Magruder's well known words, that there is no harm in the asking.[31]

B. Statutory Language

The California solicitation statute states:

§647. Every person who commits any one of the following acts is guilty of disorderly conduct, a misdemeanor: (a) Who slicits anyone to engage in or who engages in lewd or dissolute conduct in any public place or in any place open to the public or exposed to public view.

Though the purpose of the requirement of persistent importuning in the original English Act was to direct the criminal sanction to those who threatened a breach of the peace by harassing passers–by, that requirement is not part of the California law. Breach of the peace has not been the rationale used to suppress homosexual solicitations; rather, California courts have focused on what is assumed to be the disgust engendered in the minds of "innocent bystanders" and the affront to some purported standard of decency.[32]

This reasoning runs counter to the more realistic recommendations of the American Law Institutes's Model Penal Code and of the Wolfenden Committee in England. Both groups rejected the use of criminal law to deter sexual behavior because it is "sinful, morally wrong, or objectionable for reasons of conscience, or of religious or cultural tradition." Such deterrence is the prerogative of religious and social bodies and not of the state.[33] If private morality is the "distinctive concern" of spiritual authorities,[34] the question becomes how to regulate public manifestations of that private morality.

Solicitation occurs at the juncture of speech and behavior that, although public, may be protected by the Constitution, with sexual activity that may be punished as "lewd," "dissolute," or "lascivious" if engaged in in public.

"Lewd" and "dissolute" have been variously defined, never with precision. *Black's Law Dictionary* offers the following: "obscene," "that form of immorality which has relation to moral impurity," and "loose in morals." Definitions derive from vagrancy statutes, which once provided a legal means for harrassing individuals considered unsavory or immoral. The law permitted the creation and prosecution of such "status" crimes, for judges were seen as guardians of a certain, not very tolerant, moral ethic. These crimes are now held to be unconstitutional because of their inherent vagueness, the likelihood of discriminatory enforcement, and the lack of notice as to the nature of prohibited conduct.[35]

"Engaging" is defined legally as "employing or involving oneself in," or "taking part in." Generally, the term denotes more than a single act or transaction, according to *Black's Law Dictionary*. Under the California solicitation statute, the term may be construed to mean doing the prohibited act or acts, or any attempt to do them. Apparently included would be any word or act which, in the eyes of an observer, would signal involvement in "lewd or dissolute" conduct.[36] Thus, in discussing the constitutional limitations inherent in the language of solicitation statutes, attention must be directed toward guarantees of freedom of speech,[37] due process requirements, and the contours of the as yet emerging right of privacy.[38]

The discussion here will focus on the California statutes and the question of their constitutional validity. Though similar statutes have been challenged elsewhere, few cases are reported.[39] One exceptional jurisdiction is the District of Columbia, whose solicitation statutes were struck down initially on the grounds of due process, free speech, and privacy.[40] In each case the Court of Appeals reversed, saying that "lewd and immoral purposes" had been uniformly and exclusively applied to sodomy, and that the dismissals were groundless, and finally admonishing the trial judge that the law is a structure of rules, "not an amorphous jelly."[41] However, when faced with a challenge to the words "any other lewd, obscene or indecent act," the Court concluded that the words betrayed all the classic defects of vagueness and had "almost limitless application."[42] Thus, in the District of Columbia, the words "any lewd . . . sexual proposal" pass constitutional muster but the words "any other lewd . . . act" do not. The result is a degree of hair-splitting that contributes little to the ordered development of precedent.

C. CONSTITUTIONAL LIMITATIONS

(1) Freedom of Speech

The courts have devoted a great deal of attention to delineating the line between speech that deserves constitutional protection and speech that may properly be regulated or proscribed. Although all speech is presumptively protected, it may lose its constitutional protection where it consists of what the courts call "fighting words," that is, expressions "which by their very utterance inflict injury or tend to incite an immediate breach of the peace."[43]

This exception has been applied very narrowly by the United States Supreme Court, which recently struck down a statute that made unlawful the use of obscene or opprobrious language towards members of the police. The Court said that such language would be unlikely to provoke a violent reaction from the officer, who could be expected to exercise restraint.[44]

If "opprobrious" language to a law enforcement officer is protected, it would seem that the ambiguous[45] language of most homosexual solicitations would not come within the "fighting words" exception to the First Amendment. This point of view is strengthened by the fact that, almost without exception, prosecuted "solicitations" are those in which the only "victim" is a police decoy and under conditions where no one else is present or where there is an expectation that no one else will hear.

Another exception to the protection of speech is where the speech involved consists of obscene depictions. Here, in particular, the content, form, and audience involved are critical in determining whether the matter is constitutionally protected.[46] The familiar judicial definitions of obscenity as "prurient," "potentially offensive," and lacking "serious" value are of little assitance because the solicitation statute punishes *any* solicitation for lewd conduct, even in the most polite terms.

The California Court of Appeal has upheld the constitutionality of Section 647(a), declaring that since the state may punish the commission of an "obscene act," and since such an act may "manifest itself . . . in the oral description of conduct,"[47]

the solicitation (in and of itself) of an obscene act will reasonably be deemed obscene conduct or at least a written or oral description of obscene conduct and therefore beyond First Amendment protection.[48]

To reach this decision, the court relied on a previous California case holding (in the context of theatrical performances) that the terms "lewd" and "dissolute" are synonymous with "obscene," and that solicitations are synonymous with descriptions.[49]

In a case involving public masturbation, another California court, though unhappy with the definition of "obscene" discussed above, was unable to be more precise and finally relied on the words "lustful, lascivious, unchaste, wanton, or loose in morals and conduct" to define "lewd and dissolute."[50]

Obviously, not all lustful or "loose" conduct is unlawful. A definition encompassing all solicitations for such conduct includes within its terms speech which is constitutionally protected, and is overbroad "on its face." Generally the audience to the "solicitation" is carefully limited and almost always is a single decoy officer. Thus, the statute is overbroad as applied to the intimate personal communications often prosecuted. Holding a similar ordinance unconstitutional, the Ohio Court of Appeals stated:

Even though the ordinance deals with invitations to engage in sexual activity, the constitutional problem is not solved in favor of the ordinance. Since sexual activity is illegal only under specific circumstances, and since the ordinance is not limited to illegal sexual activity and since an invitation to sexual activity is not, necessarily, obscene, the ordinance is not limited by its own wording to "obscene" speech.

In the same way in which invitations to engage in sexual activity are not, necessarily, obscene, those invitations are not, necessarily, fighting words. In fact those invitations could easily be classified as loving words.

This analysis would suggest that the ordinance is unconstitutional since it is not limited to fighting or obscene words.[51]

(2) Vagueness

The due process clause of the Constitution has been held to prohibit laws whose meanings are unclear or whose coverage is uncertain. This "vagueness" doctrine protects the citizens' right to plan their actions so as to avoid criminal liability, guards against arbitrary and discriminatory enforcement, and provides a buffer zone to protect the full exercise of First Amendment freedoms.[52]

The meaning of the words of the solicitation laws is obscure.[53] Though in extreme circumstances, such as public masturbation, the courts have had no difficulty in upholding such statutes, the situation is seldom so clear-cut. For example, "public place," within the meaning of section 647 ranges from a business open to the public[54] to the area in front of a house, whether a driveway, lawn, or front porch.[55] The court in *People v. Silva* held that solicitation was prohibited regardless of where the solicited acts were to be performed.[56] It would seem reasonable to conclude that persons of ordinary intelligence could not have received "fair warning" that a discussion in a gay bar, or even on their own doorstep, might result in a misdemeanor conviction.

Further, since "sexual motivation" has been held to be the prime element of "lewdness," this determinant is left to the subjective perceptions — and, inevitably, to the personal value systems — of police, judges and juries. This subjectivity is nowhere more dangerous than in sexual matters. The long history of homophobia in the United States practically assures that the law will be applied to vindicate the private moral views of those who apply it. An apt illustration of the vagueness of California's solicitation law under this test is the attempt by the court in *People* v. *Williams* to demonstrate the contrary. The *Williams* court concluded that the terms "lewd and dissolute" were not vague, because juries would inevitably interpret them "according to prevailing notions of what . . . conduct fits the description."[57] In one of the rare decisions where this type of statutory language was held to lack the requisite definiteness, a Michigan federal judge ruled that subjectivity was inherent

in that whether an act is "lustful," "dissolute," "libidinous," or "lascivious" depends on the actor's social, moral and cultural bias. There are no objective standards to measure whether proposed conduct is lewd.[58]

Moreover, the decriminalization of private, adult, consensual conduct should place those relations outside the ambit of the solicitation laws. This was the position taken by the State in a case now under consideration by the California Supreme Court, *Pryor* v. *Municipal Court.*[59] The argument would avoid invalidating the law by construing it to apply only to solicitations for sex acts that are themselves illegal. Whether the Court will accept this view, or strike down the statute in its entirety, remains to be seen.

(3) Privacy

The right to privacy "emanates" from the Fourth Amendment freedom from unreasonable searches and seizures and from the First Amendment freedom of speech. In a landmark decision, *Katz* v. *United States*, the Court held that "the Fourth Amendment protects people, not places." The protections of the Fourth Amendment are not lost simply because an individual leaves the privacy of the home.[60] The relevant constitutional question revolves around *when* people are protected from impermissible intrustions upon privacy interests.

In California the test was stated succinctly in *People* v. *Sneed*:

The basic test as to whether there has been an unconstitutional invasion of privacy is whether the person has exhibited a subjective expectation of privacy which is objectively reasonable and, if so, whether that expectation has been violated by reasonable governmental intrusion.[61]

This test must be supplemented by stricter requirements where freedom of speech is involved. Words of intimacy would generally seem to have an attendant expectation of privacy, whether they are spoken in a "public" place or not.

In nearly all sexual solicitation cases the defendant has a subjective expectation of privacy. Given that homosexual solicitations are usually "cautious pursuits" undertaken in places or manners not normally observed by those likely to be offended, it would seem that most such expectations of privacy are objectively reasonable. A recent California case held that even the "semi-public" nature of a university classroom does not preclude a Fourth Amendment expectation of privacy deserving of protection.[62] An earlier case held that patrons of an open toilet stall had the right to assume that no clandestine police observation was taking place.[63]

It is within this context that the reasonableness of the police decoy and undercover operations must be examined. Usually the decoy makes certain remarks or gestures, or wears distinctive clothing, intended to lead homosexual men into conversations which suggest that solicitation would be favorably received. Technically these police tactics do not constitute "entrapment," because the officer or decoy does not actually suggest criminal activity. However, where the authorities consciously provide an atmosphere conducive to the uttering of words of solicitation — and no bystanders are present — many would conclude that an objective expectation of privacy is present.

IV. ENFORCEMENT ISSUES

The stereotype frequently invoked by courts, of a brazen and flagrantly homosexual male accosting and affronting innocent bystanders, is largely a myth. As newspaper articles[64] consistently confirm, homosexual persons who openly display their sexuality risk taunts and violent assault even in "tolerant" urban areas. It is not surprising, then, that most homosexual cruising and solicitations are unobtrusive and that arrests are possible only through the diligent use of undercover agents and decoys.

The landmark *U.C.L.A. Law Review* study of homosexuality stated:

(I)t is questionable whether convictions should be based exclusively on the oral testimony of the arresting officer. No crime is easier to charge or harder to disprove than the sex offense. In addition to lack of corroboration, the solicitation may be equivocal or unindicative of a firm intent to consummate the solicited

act. When prosecutions are limited to credibility contests between defendants and arresting officers the likelihood of miscarriages of justice is evident . . . [65]

The U.C.L.A. investigators found that complaints from private citizens about homosexual solicitations were practically unknown. Likewise, a more recent study[66] in Los Angeles indicates that complaints from members of the general public about conduct in violation of the solicitation laws are virtually nonexistent. Of the 662 arrests studied, 642 were made by plainclothes policemen, and 15 by uniformed officers. Only five involved complaints from private citizens, of whom two were actually private security officers. The remaining three complaints by private individuals were not for homosexual solicitation, but for lewd conduct of a heterosexual character. Both the original and a follow-up study[67] confirmed that although numerous private citizens file complaints for indecent exposure of a heterosexual nature, the complainants in all the homosexual conduct cases were plainclothes vice officers.

Instead of going to trial, most defendants plea-bargained. On the average, homosexual men received a $100 fine and 18 to 24 months' probation, with various conditions imposed. The vast majority of cases were disposed of through the use of the trespassing statute. A double standard was revealed in that heterosexual persons, where charged, often received a less serious breach of the peace conviction or a dismissal.

It seems fair to conclude that homosexual solicitations do not present a threat serious enough to the public peace or welfare to justify the methods of enforcement required to make arrests. Even a police officer versed in the intricacies of the *Williams* and *Silva* cases is faced with conflicting and uncertain meanings of "lewd and dissolute" and "sexual motivation." Obviously, the judge or jury in an individual case is in no better position to make judgments under legislative standards that are so subjective. This uncertainty provides arresting officers and prosecutors with manifold opportunities for arbitrary and discriminatory enforcement.

In Los Angeles, studies have found that police officers equated the phrase "lewd and dissolute conduct" with "homosexual conduct." Any display of affection between males that hinted of sexuality would also fall under most officers' conceptions of criminality. The situation has now changed with the adoption of more restrictive prosecutorial guidelines by the Los Angeles City Attorney. Among these guidelines are evidentiary limitations requiring aggressiveness by the solicitor and specific details related to a public sex act; the use of the battery offense where there is non-consensual touching; and no filing of charges for consensual touching unless the complainant is known and the offensiveness was observed.[68]

In San Francisco, although charges continue to be filed in increasing numbers against females and males for prostitution solicitations, almost no charges are filed for noncommercial sexual solicitations.

These limited, moderate reforms do not exist in most parts of California, where the arrest and prosecution of homosexual men for cruising and soliciting continues unabated. Depending on the locality in which it occurs, the outcome of a single solicitation may vary from no penalty at all to conviction and indefinite registration as a sex offender.

V. SEX OFFENDER REGISTRATION

California law requires a person convicted of solicitation to register with the chief of police of the city, or with the sheriff of the county, in which the offender lives. Registration consists of a written statement, fingerprints, and a photograph. Under penalty of a misdemeanor, the so-called "sex offender" is required to notify law enforcement officials after any change of residence address. The statute specifies that the information "shall not be open to inspection by the public or by any person other than a regularly employed peace or other law enforcement officer."

Though law enforcement officials claim that this requirement is a mere "administrative" procedure to keep track of recidivists and is not "punishment" at all, sex offender registration laws have a significant impact on the individual. The registration requirement is a permanent intrusion into the affected person's autonomy, liberty and privacy, and can be a humiliating reminder of what may have been a relatively harmless misadventure. Although there are supposed requirements of limited access to these records, identified photographs taken from the files have been shown to individuals complaining of sex offenses in San Francisco.[69] The imposition of this requirement results in a disabling status without any opportunity for the individual affected to have a determination as to whether he is, in fact, a recidivist and a lifelong danger to society. Although the ostensible purpose of registration is to prevent recidivism, many sex offenses with high rates of recidivism, such as rape and child molestation, are not included within the requirement. These latter offenses are more often committed by men in heterosexual situations, indication once again of a discriminatory impact on homosexual persons.[70]

The most serious constitutional question here is whether such a procedure is in reality "cruel and unusual punishment" prohibited by the Eighth Amendment.[71] In *People v. Anderson*,[72] the California Supreme Court ruled that the death penalty statute then in force violated the constitutional mandate against cruel and unusual punishment. The *Anderson* test for determining whether a punishment is cruel and unusual is "whether the punishment affronts contemporary standards of decency;" that is, "the evolving standards of decency that mark the progress of a maturing society." The legalization of consensual sexual acts is a significant indication that, in the states where it has occurred, standards of decency regarding homosexual behavior are changing in the direction of greater tolerance of homosexuality.

Another California case[73] formulated a three-part test for cruel and unusual punishment based on disproportionality. Where punishment is of excessive severity for ordinary offenses, it might be held cruel and unusual after consideration of: (1) the nature of the offense, (2) the severity of the punishment as compared to that for more serious crimes, and (3) the disparity of treatment when contrasted with punishment for the same offense in other jurisdictions. The California solicitation laws retain the minor offense character of the vagrancy statutes from which they are descended, both in an absolute sense and when compared to other sex offenses. The criminal behavior involved in solicitation is usually victimless, consisting of nothing more harmful to society than an invitation to sex. Further, as the range of activity open to prosecution includes casual "cruising" and merely ambiguous dialogues culminating in invitations for further interaction, the registration requirement is clearly a disproportionate punishment for these activities.

Registration, where applied to convictions for solicitation, is excessive when compared with the punishments for similar crimes. Registration is imposed for crimes such as forcible rape, but not for solicitation for prostitution nor for certain sexual crimes involving children, sending a minor to a saloon, maintaining a house of prostitution, child pornography, pimping and pandering, bestiality, nor sexual intercourse with an unconscious female.

The most recent study of registration statutes of cities over 50,000 in population was reported in 1969.[74] Only 13 out of 384 cities surveyed had sex offender registration ordinances. By 1976, only four states required registration for serious sex offenses. Ohio required registration only after conviction for two or more offenses in separate transactions. Nevada limited registration to sex offenses classified as felonies. Only Arizona had a registration requirement comparable to California's.

VI. CONCLUSION

Homosexual "cruising" is, paradoxically, less general than commonly supposed, while also being an apparently essential element of the gay male milieu. Just as it is essential, such behavior is also quite diverse, encompassing a wide range of speech and activity.

Though homosexuality occurs in nearly all societies, there have been consistent attempts to control it in some manner. The controls in California are presently based on solicitation statutes and on laws proscribing "lewd, dissolute or lascivious" conduct. The language of such statutes is constitutionally objectionable on the grounds that it violates freedom of speech, due process requirements regarding vagueness, and the emerging right of privacy. These constitutional infirmities manifest themselves in arbitrary and discriminatory enforcement against homosexual males. Further, the imposition of a sex offender registration requirement for solicitation is inequitable, when considered in comparison with other crimes.

Judicial, legislative, and administrative reforms are being sought by newly emergent gay rights advocates to eliminate the presently unjust system of control of homosexual behavior. As the movement for recognition of the rights of lesbians and gay men increases in visibility and political consciousness, it will become more difficult to enforce inequitable statutes effectively.

The growing assertion of the rights of gay persons must be seen, of course, against the movement for increased repression by the "new and radical right." The pressure to return to a simplistic morality can only be countered successfully by strong and successful coalitions of all those who are threatened by repression. The eventual elimination of the solicitation laws depends on the extent to which fundamentalist morality gains a dominant position as the justification for law. Given the diversity of homosexual desires and the variety of styles and manners of "cruising," it is unlikely any statute could be devised that would prohibit all such behavior and still be constitutional, as that term is presently understood.

FOOTNOTES

1. J. Rechy, *The Sexual Outlaw* 100 (1977) (italics omitted).
2. D. J. West, *Homosexuality Re-Examined* 123 (1977).
3. A. Karlen, *Sexuality and Homosexuality* (1971).
4. W. Churchill, *Homosexual Behavior Among Males* 156 (1967).
5. A.C. Kinsey, *et al.*, *Sexual Behavior in the Human Male* (1948).
6. *Ibid.*; A.C. Kinsey *et al.*, *Sexual Behavior in the Human Female* (1953).
7. D.J. West, *supra* n. 2; at 241-42.
8. M. Weinberg and C. Williams, *Male Homosexuals: Their Problems and Adaptations* 83-84 (1974).
9. A. Karlen, *supra* n. 3, at 543; A. Bell and M. Weinberg, *Homosexualities: A Study of Human Diversity* 79 (1978).
10. *Ibid.* at 73.
11. *Ibid.* at 79.
12. *Ibid.* at 80.
13. J. Rechy, *supra* n. 1, at 28.
14. A. Bell and M. Weinberg, *supra* n. 9, at 74; *cf.* W. Churchill, *supra* n. 4, at 55.
15. E. Goffman, *Encounters* 7 (1961).
16. *Ibid.* at 7.
17. C.A. Tripp, *The Homosexual Matrix* 144 (1975).

18. *Ibid.* at 142; *see* A. Bell and M. Weinberg, *supra* n. 9, at 101.
19. C.A. Tripp, *supra* n. 17, at 147.
20. M. Hoffman, *The Gay World* 177 (paper ed. 1969).
21. J. Rechy, *supra* n. 1, at 194, 233-34.
22. A. Bell and M. Weinberg, *supra* n. 9, at 230.
23. Project Report, "The Consensual Adult Homosexual and the Law: An Empirical Study of Enforcement and Administration in Los Angeles County," 13 *U.C.L.A. L. Rev.* 643 (1966).
24. C. A. Tripp, *supra* n. 17, at 147.
25. M. Hoffman, *supra* n. 20, at 57.
26. *Black's Law Dictionary* 1564 (4th ed. 1951).
27. Only seven states (Alabama, Alaska, Hawaii, Illinois, New Hampshire, New York, and Utah) have comprehensive solicitation statutes covering solicitation of any crime. Three states (Louisiana, Vermont, and Wisconsin) punish solicitation to commit a felony; one (Idaho) punishes solicitation of misdemeanors; and only one (California) enumerates the offenses, solicitation of which is punishable. *See* W. LaFave and A. Scott, *Handbook on Criminal Law* 415-16 (1972).
28. *Ibid.* at 416.
29. Model Penal Code, art. 5, Comment (Tent. Draft No. 10, 1960).
30. For this observation and many other insights I am indebted to research of the National Committee for Sexual Civil Liberties. *See,* in particular, A. Warner, *Non-Commercial Sexual Solicitation: The Case for Judicial Invalidation,* 4 Sexual L. Rptr. 1 (1978).
31. W. Prosser, *Law of Torts* 51 (4th ed. 1971), *quoting* Magruder, "Mental and Emotional Disturbance in the Law of Torts," 49 *Harv. L. Rev.* 1033, 1055 (1936).
32. *People* v. *Dudley,* 250 Cal. App. 2d Supp. 955, 58 Cal. Rptr. 557, 559 (1967).
33. *Report of the Departmental Committee on Homosexual Offenses and Prostitution* (The Wolfenden Report) CMD No. 247, paragraph 14, at 21 (paper ed. 1964).
34. Model Penal Code §207.1-6, note 9, at 277-78 (Tent. Draft No. 4, 1955).
35. *In re Newbern,* 53 Cal. 2d 786, 350 P. 2d 116, 3 Cal. Rptr. 364 (1960).
36. Interpreting a Kansas City, Missouri, solicitation statute, a state apellate court held that the offense of soliciting does not require "any particular form of words, and, in fact, may be committed by gesture alone . . ." *Kansas City* v. *Plumb,* 419, S.W. 2d 457, 459 (Mo. App. 1967).
37. Congress shall make no law respecting an establishment of religion, or prohibiting the free exercise thereof; or abridging the freedom of speech, or of the press; or of the right of the people peaceably to assemble, and to petition the Government for a redress of grievances. *U.S. Constitution, Amendment I.*
38. *Griswold* v. *Connecticut,* 381 U.S. 479 (1965). The Court's opinion, written by Mr. Justice Douglas, saw the right as a "penumbra" emanating from certain specifics in the Bill of Rights. The concurring opinion of Mr. Justice Goldberg (in which Chief Justice Warren and Mr. Justice Brennan joined) found the right "retained by the People" under the ninth amendment. Justices Harlan and White found the right "implicit in the concept of ordered liberty" under the due process clause.
39. *See* Annot., 77 A.L.R. 3rd 519 (Solicitation).
40. *U.S.* v. *Carson,* 319 A. 2d 329 (D.C. App. 1974). *See, also, Riley* v. *U.S.,* 298 A. 2d 228 (D.C. App. 1972), *cert. denied,* 414 U.S. 840 (1973), *District of Columbia* v. *Garcia,* 335 A. 2d 217 (D.C. App.), *cert denied,* 423 U.S. 894(1975); *U.S.* v. *Dumas,* 327 A. 2d 826 (D.C. App. 1974). Some cases have relied on the doctrines of equal protection and cruel and unusual punishment.
41. *U.S.* v. *Kenyon,* 354 A.2d 861, 862 (D.C. App. 1976), *quoting Mitchell* v. *U.S.,* 259 F.2d 787, 791-92 (D.C. Cir. 1958).

42. *District of Columbia* v. *Walters,* 319 A. 2d 332, 335 (D.C. App.) *appeal dismissed and cert. denied,* 419 U.S. 1065 (1974).
43. *Chaplinsky* v. *New Hampshire,* 315 U.S. 568, 572 (1942).
44. *Lewis* v. *City of New Orleans,* 415 U.S. 130, 132 (1974).
45. Rechy offers the following:

> *Now a very handsome dark young man drives by in a mangled sportscar.*
> *"You got a place?" he asks Jim.*
>
> . . .
>
> *"Yeah—just a few minutes from here," he says . . .*
> *"Follow you there?"*
> *"Sure."*

J. Rechy, *supra* n. 1, at 65.
46. *Miller* v. *California,* 413 U.S. 15 (1973).
47. *Kaplan* v. *California,* 413 U.S. 115, 119 (1973).
48. *Silva* v. *Municipal Court,* 40 Cal. App. 3d 733, 737, 115 Cal. Rptr. 655 (1968). *Contra, State of Ohio* v. *Phipps,* No. C-76886 (March 19, 1978), 4 Sexual L. Rptr. 26. In this case the Ohio Court of Appeal voided an Ohio statute that prohibited homosexual solicitations where the solicitor was "offensive" to the other person or "reckless" in that regard. Following the appointment of two new judges to that court, the dissent in *Phipps* became a majority which specifically disapproved the prior holding that the statute violated First Amendment rights to freedom of speech and Fourteenth Amendment vagueness standards.
    Nevertheless, the new decision, *State* v. *Faulk,* No. C-77486 (Sept. 13, 1978), held that the state could not prohibit homosexual solicitation while permitting heterosexual solicitation without violating the Equal Protection clause of the Fourteenth Amendment, an issue not raised in *Phipps.* The dissenting opinion in *Phipps* is represented in full at 4 Sexual L. Rptr. 64. *Cf. District of Columbia* v. *Garcia, supra* n. 39, where the court held that since the proposed sexual act was lewd or obscene, the character of the particular words did not matter.
49. *In re Giannini,* 69 Cal. 2d 563, 446 P. 2d 535, 72 Cal. Rptr. 655 (1968).
50. *People* v. *Williams,* 59 Cal. App. 3d 225, 130 Cal. Rptr. 460 (1976).
51. *City of Columbus* v. *Scott,* 353 N.E. 2d 858, 861 (1975) (citations omitted).
52. *See Grayned* v. *City of Rockford,* 408 U.S. 104, 108-109 (1972).
53. Though the United States Supreme Court has used the word "lewd," *Chaplinsky* v. *New Hampshire, supra* n. 37, and upheld a federal obscenity statute using that word, *Roth* v. *United States,* 354 U.S. 476 (1956), it has never particularly defined or discussed it in terms of due process. However, the Court recently upheld against a vagueness challenge a Tennessee statute proscribing "crimes against nature." *Rose* v. *Locke,* 423 U.S. 48, 52 (1975).
54. *People* v. *Blatt,* 23 Cal. App. 3d 148, 99 Cal. Rptr. 855 (1972). Even a closed room in such a business would qualify as "public". *In Re Steinke,* 2 Cal. App. 3d 569, 82 Cal. Rptr. 789 (1969). Another California court defined "public" as "[c]ommon to all or many; general; . . . open to common, or general use, participation, enjoyment, etc. . . . ." *In Re Zorn,* 59 Cal. 2d 650, 652, 30 Cal. Rptr. 811, 812 (1963) (citations omitted).

55. *People* v. *Olson,* 18 Cal. App. 3d 592, 96 Cal. Rptr. 132 (1971).
56. *Silva* v. *Municipal Court,* 40 Cal. App. 3d 733, 736, 115 Cal. Rptr. 479, 480 (1974).
57. *People* v. *Williams,* 59 Cal. App. 3d 225, 231, 130 Cal. Rptr. 460, 463 (1976). *Cf. Anderson* v. *State,* 562 P. 2d 351 (1977); *District of Columbia* v. *Garcia, supra* n. 39, where the use of the word "lewd" was upheld when joined with words providing a definite context giving the word meaning.
58. *Morgan* v. *City of Detroit,* 389 F. Supp. 922, 930 (E.D. Mich. 1975).
59. *Pryor* v. *Municipal Court,* L.A. No. 30901 (Cal., argued June 6, 1978).
60. *Katz* v. *United States,* 389 U.S. 347, 351 (1967).
61. *People* v. *Sneed,* 32 Cal. App. 3d 535, 540, 108 Cal. Rptr. 146, 149 (1973).
62. *White* v. *Davis,* 13 Cal. 3d 757, 533 P. 2d 222, 120 Cal. Rptr. 94 (1975).
63. *People* v. *Triggs,* 8 Cal. 3d 884, 506 P. 2d 232, 106 Cal. Rptr. 408 (1973). The right of privacy has been asserted in connection with "personal intimacies" protected in several United States Supreme Court cases. *(E.g., Roe* v. *Wade,* 410 U.S. 113 (1973) (right of a woman to terminate her pregnancy); *Stanley* v. *Georgia,* 394 U.S. 557 (1969) (right to possess obscene materials in the home); *Griswold* v. *Connecticut,* 381 U.S. 479 (1965) (right to use contraceptives in privacy of marital bedroom). But the right has not been extended beyond family and home. *Doe* v. *Commonwealth's Attorney,* 403 F. Supp. 1199 (E.D. Va. 1975), *aff'd mem.,* 425 U.S. 901 (1976). Such was also the opinion of the Court in *United States* v. *Buck,* 342 A. 2d 48 (D.C. App. 1075). There the court reaffirmed its rejection of privacy claims for vehicles, bedrooms, or closed cubicles in gay health clubs or bookstores, as well as for a "public wooded area" where participants believed themselves unobserved because of "the density of the foliage." 342 A.2d at 49.
64. *E.g.,* Bell, "Hunting Gays in Central Park: Midnight Rambling Takes a Bloody Turn," 23 *Village Voice* No. 29, July 24, 1978, p. 1.
65. Project Report, *supra* n. 23, at 695.
66. B. Copilow and T. Coleman, *Report on the Enforcement of Section 647 (a) of the California Penal Code by the Los Angeles Police Department* (1972).
67. C.R. Toy, Update: *Enforcement of Section 647 (a) of the California Penal Code by the Los Angeles Police Department* (1974).
68. *See, Los Angeles Prosecutor Reforms Guidelines on Lewd Conduct Cases,* 3 Sexual L. Rptr. 25, 36 (1977).
69. Interview with Jan S. Rice, student, San Francisco State University, California, May 20, 1978. Though the police claim that such records are available only to those "entitled by law" (conversation with Lt. Long, San Francisco Police Dept., Aug. 30, 1978), pictures from the registration records are used in show-ups and to assist victims in identifying perpetrators of assaults, etc. Lt. Long could not account for the fact that both picture and name were presented in the case cited.
70. *Oregon Task Force Preliminary Report,* 3 Sexual L. Rptr. 39, 52-53 (1977).
71. *See, Sex Offender Registration for Section 647 Disorderly Conduct is Cruel and Unusual Punishment,* 13 San Diego L. Rev. 391 (1976). A recent California case has challenged the constitutionality of California Penal Code Section 290: *In re Anders.* Crim. No. 20198 (Ca., awaiting decision).
72. *People* v. *Anderson,* 6 Cal. 3d 628, 493 P. 2d 880, 100 Cal. Rptr. 152, *cert. den.,* 406 U.S. 958 (1972).
73. *In re Lynch,* 8 Cal. 3d 410, 503 P. 2d 921, 105 Cal. Rptr. 217 (1972).
74. R.H. Dreher and L. Kammler, *Criminal Registration Statutes and Ordinances in the United States — A Compilation* § IV, Table II (Monograph for Center for the Study of Crime, Delinquency and Corrections, Southern Illinois University, Carbondale, Ill., 1969).

THE HOMOSEXUAL PERSON IN THE MILITARY AND IN NATIONAL SECURITY EMPLOYMENT

Jerel McCrary, J.D.
Lewis Gutierrez

INTRODUCTION

Gay people in America encounter a society whose dominant traditions and attitudes cast them as pariahs. In employment situations, this frequently means that we must hide our lives during the working day and live in constant fear of discovery and the loss of our jobs.

Employment discrimination in the private sector is often discreet. It is the rare private employer today who codifies anti-gay prejudice as a written exclusionary policy. But officials of the United States government have not hesitated to express the opinion that homosexual men and women are psychopathic by definition and represent a threat to the efficiency of the military and to the security of classified information. The gay person in the military or in national security employment will encounter a panoply of regulations and procedures specifically designed to screen out and remove all homosexual personnel from these areas.

The purpose of this chapter is to explore the attitude of the government toward gay people in the military and in national security employment, to see how this attitude has been translated into official policy, to view challenges to these policies, and to note how challenges have been received by courts and administrative agencies.

I. HOMOSEXUALITY AND THE MILITARY

A. An Historical Overview of Homosexuality and the Military

The prohibition against homosexual persons serving in the military is not unique to twentieth century America, but the vehemence with which

---

Jerel McCrary is in private law practice in San Francisco, where he also serves as a volunteer attorney for Gay Rights Advocates. He graduated with a B.A. in History from Stanford University in 1974 and received his J.D. from Hastings College of the Law in 1977. The author wishes to express his thanks to Jeffrey Jackl, a student at the Stanford Law School, for his assistance with this article.

this policy has been pursued is nearly unparalleled in history. Many societies have regarded the presence of homosexual individuals in their armed forces as simply an unspoken fact of life. Indeed, some aggressive military cultures, such as the Dorian Greeks of ancient times[1] and the Japanese samurai of the middle ages,[2] deliberately encouraged erotic relations between men as conducive to military loyalty and prowess.[3] And throughout the height of the Roman empire, male bisexuality was considered the norm.[4]

Perhaps the outstanding instance of a Christian society in which military leadership was largely in the hands of homosexual officials was seventeenth–century France. The aristocracy, from which military leadership was drawn, enjoyed a kind of legal immunity from sanctions against homosexuality. Although Louis XIV was personally hostile to homosexuality as a lifestyle, a remarkable number of distinguished French generals were homosexual or bisexual.[5] So common was homosexuality among the military elite and the French court that Louis's advisor, Louvois, restrained him from taking measures against it.[6]

The historical record bears proof that homosexual men have played an important role in the military life of numerous nations—particularly as military leaders.[7] Many twentieth-century societies have also come to the conclusion that homosexual soldiers should not automatically be excluded from military service. Italy, Japan, Taiwan, Thailand, Republic of the Philippines, Norway, Spain, Belgium, and the Netherlands have no specific prohibitions against homosexual persons in the armed services. Countries with minor prohibitions include Germany, Turkey, Greece, and Denmark.[8]

But in the United States, the policy has been to exclude all homosexual men and women from entering the military and to discharge all who are discovered. From time to time throughout United States military history, there have also been pogroms to rid the services of any homosexual persons who had escaped initial detection. One notorious example was supervised by the then Assistant Secretary of the Navy, Franklin D. Roosevelt.[9]

The Armed Forces have always displayed substantial resistance to permitting persons outside the social mainstream to serve within their ranks. Throughout the second World War there were bitter debates as to whether blacks should be integrated into regiments and battalions occupied exclusively by whites. While the debates eventually ended with acceptance of integration, the language that emanated from the military opposition to such plans presents an interesting basis for comparison with official pronouncements in the present debate. In seeking to justify a refusal to accept racial integration, the Army's public response ran as follows:

. . . Now the Army's duty is to fight battles and win wars. Therefore, the Army must maintain morale in the ranks and use its manpower with maximum efficiency. Integration would lower morale and impair efficiency. Whites just will not serve with blacks, and even if they would, it is not possible to train and use Negroes in highly skilled jobs. The Army must take the country as it is. It must accept social patterns and keep abreast of changes, but is not an instrument for social experimentation. [10]

Similar arguments were used by the military to oppose the Women's Armed Services Integration Act of 1948 [11] and the recent attempts to admit women to the military academies. [12] Thus, contentions that the presence of gay people in the service would disturb efficiency and morale have a familiar ring. [13]

Despite the fact that official policy has long called for elimination of homosexual individuals from the services, the only "uniform" regulation regarding "deviate" sexual behavior is Article 125 of the Uniform Code of Military Justice. Article 125 deals with sodomy generally. It establishes a procedure for courts-martial and provides for punishment of up to 16 years with hard labor upon conviction. [14] Ordinarily, court-martial proceedings are not used to process homosexual soldiers out of the service, except under extraordinary circumstances, such as sodomy with a minor. [15]

B. The Administrative Process of the U.S. Armed Forces

Separation from military service is usually accomplished by means of an administrative hearing process governed by regulations promulgated by each branch of the service. Typical of administrative directives on homosexuality was Secretary of the Navy Instruction, SECNAVY 1900.9:

Homosexuals and other sexual deviates are military liabilities who cannot be tolerated in a military organization. On developing and documenting cases involving homosexual conduct, commanding officers should be keenly aware that homosexuals are security and reliability risks who discredit themselves and the Navy by their homosexual conduct. Their prompt separation from the service is essential. . . [16]

The naval policy as amended in 1978 appears to indicate that elimination of homosexual sailors and officers is no longer mandatory. The regulation states, however, that "The presence of such a member in a military establishment seriously impairs combat readiness, efficiency, security, and morale." [17] As of February 1, 1978, Army Regulations did not reflect any change. [18]

Within the administrative system, homosexual members may be classified, for "flexibility in department handling" according to offense commited (if an offense at all).[19] The Navy's classifications are composed roughly as follows:

CLASS I. Servicemen who have committed homosexual offenses involving force, fraud, intimidation, or the seduction of a minor. These cases are usually tried by general court-martial and, if conviction ensues, sentence usually involves imprisonment, fine and punitive discharges (Dishonorable or Bad Conduct).

CLASS II. Servicemen who have willfully engaged in, or attempted to perform, homosexual acts which do not fall under the Class I category. Such persons are usually administratively processed and receive an Undesirable Discharge, though theoretically they can receive Honorable or General Discharges. The majority of homosexual persons dealt with by the military fall into this class.

CLASS III. Servicemen who exhibit, profess, or admit homosexual tendencies or associate with known homosexual others. This class also includes those who were homosexual before entering the service. The common feature of this class is that no homosexual acts or offenses have been committed while in the service. Such cases are processed administratively and can receive Honorable Discharges, though most receive either General or Undesirable Discharges.[20]

A survey by Colin Williams and Martin Weinberg in 1971 indicated that the majority of gay personnel identified by military authorities were reported by civilians or other soldiers.[21] In a recent case, Commander Gary Hess of Santa Barbara, while serving as a School Board member, was reported to the military by two unsuccessful political candidates who had been questioned by him regarding their stands on consensual adult sexual behavior.[22]

The interrogation process, which immediately follows discovery, is often so rigorous that an accused will be frightened into waiving critical procedural rights. Respondents to the survey by Williams and Weinberg complained they had been misinformed, or not informed at all, of their rights. One of the respondents to that survey summed up the procedure thus:

I saw a chaplain and he said to tell the truth and the Judge Advocate of the base told me I could not get any legal advice until the investigation was complete. I found out now that's a lie.

I signed a statement for the O.S.I. (Office of Special Investigation). I received notice of trial and was assigned a lawyer. He asked me (about cooperating) and he said, "You've already hung yourself."[23]

All of this trauma is merely a prelude to the formal separation process.

The formal procedure usually begins with notice to the accused of investigation of charges of homosexuality, or notice of discharge proceedings before a Board of Officers. The accused has 15 days to answer the complaint, and to request a hearing with counsel or to waive those rights. A board, consisting of three to five officers, is then chosen. The board is not confined in its deliberations by strict rules of evidence, such as the prohibitions against "hearsay." On the basis of the "preponderance of the evidence" as presented, the board recommends retention or discharge. In the latter case, it also prescribes the nature of the discharge to be given. After review of the proceedings for legal sufficiency by the Judge Advocate General's office, the case is sent to the accused's Commanding Officer, who may either affirm the decision or upgrade it (i.e., grant a discharge more favorable than that granted by the Board of Officers or retain the defendant.) The Commanding Officer may not give a less favorable ruling. At this point, the defendant, if officially discharged, can appeal to either a Military Discharge Review Board or the Board of Corrections for Military Records (BCMR). Either body may overturn the previous decision, but final authority rests with the Secretary of the accused's particular branch of the Armed Forces. The Secretary may summarily discharge or retain the defendant regardless of prior rulings.[24]

Williams and Weinberg in their book *Homosexuals and the Military* estimate that nearly 2,000 persons per year were separated from the armed forces for homosexuality between the late 1940's and mid-1950's. Later estimates indicate that this figure is probably valid for the sixties as well.[25] In a study of 201 soldiers investigated for homosexuality in 1968, 74.6% of those discharged were given Undesirable Discharges, 16.4% were retained in the service (reason not given), 5% received General Discharges, 1.5% resigned (these were all officers), and 2.5% received other discharges.[26]

Once an accused has been brought before a Board of Officers, chances of retention or dismissal with an Honorable Discharge are minimized by the established policy approach, which regards all gay persons as detrimental to military services. Military officials have variously opined that homosexual men and women exhibit "psychopathic personalities," [27] would tend to "corrupt young recruits," [28] or should be subjected to rehabilitation programs.[29]

Regardless of the reason used to justify discharge of the homosexual soldier, one so discharged faces the consequences of that action throughout life. Considering that nearly 90% of *all* discharges are Honorable, any discharge less than Honorable carries great stigma.[30] The person so discharged will find it hard to obtain employment in many areas and may not be eligible for the military benefits available to others. For those receiving either an Undesirable or Dishonorable Discharge, the denial of benefits is established in the particular branch's administrative regulations. For a General or less-than-Honorable Discharge, the decision on benefits is left to the particular administering body (i.e., no "formal" policy exists, though the practice of denying benefits arouses suspicion about the "informal" nature of the policies.).

Even an Honorable Discharge, when given because of accusations of homosexual conduct, can carry serious ongoing consequences. In the case of Nelson v. Miller,[31] a non-commissioned officer petitioned the court to restrain the Navy from discharging him. Nelson admitted to an agent of Navy Intelligence that he had once been the victim of a "homosexual attack" while intoxicated. Although the administrative board accepted Nelson's explanation and recommended he be retained on active duty, the Chief of Naval Personnel ordered him discharged. The court denied the preliminary injunction sought by Nelson, but noted that civilian employers would be led to pry into the reasons for Nelson's discharge in order to discover why a "non-commissioned officer with as much service as ten years was leaving the service instead of remaining to obtain valuable retirement privileges . . ."[32] The court observed that Nelson could never be employed where a security clearance was required and would have to "start on an entry level at a substantially lower income."[33] Whatever the form of discharge, the discharged homosexual person may be coded as ineligible for re-enlistment and cannot obtain retirement benefits.

C. Reality Behind the Stereotype

Mr. John Everhard, writing for the *Air Force J.A.G. Bulletin*, while vigorous in his opposition to retention of homosexual persons in the military, admits that "the service records of homosexuals disclose generally that homosexuality per se has no relationship to ability to perform good military service."[34]

The public was presented with a notable example of the fallibility of the service-fostered stereotype of homosexuality in the well-publicized case of Sergeant Leonard Matlovich. Matlovich served 13 years in the U.S. Air Force, received a Bronze Star Medal and the Purple Heart, completed three tours of duty in Southeast Asia, and consistently received performance reports of the highest rating. At the time of his discharge proceedings, Matlovich was an instructor in human relations for the Air Force. There seems to have been no evidence on record denying that he had been a valuable asset to the Air Force; nevertheless, his self-proclaimed homosexuality was deemed to preclude future service.[35]

The dismissal of 15-year Navy veteran, Dennis Beller, seemed so unreasonable to Judge George Harris that he stated:

The emerging learning of numerous court cases and current psychiatric thought is that there is no basis for homosexuality or homosexual conduct per se disqualifying one from positions of trust and responsibility; rather the inquiry should be as to one's fitness for his position without regard to sexual orientation.

. . . the Navy does itself and the public little good by removing an experienced and able serviceman such as (Beller) from its ranks and it should seriously consider what interest is furthered by its decision to do so . . . It would seem more reasonable to believe that if, as the Navy posits, the great majority of its members are heterosexual, then there is a graver danger of blackmail from illicit heterosexual than homosexual liaisons.[36]

In the rare case, the service may be able to make plausible arguments to support dismissal.[37] In most cases, however, the military is unable to resort to reason and must depend on unproven generalizations about military efficiency and on stereotypes concerning the propensity of homosexual males to corrupt unsuspecting youngsters.

D. The Court System — Deference and a Glimmer of Defiance

Until 1957, the jurisdiction of federal district courts even to review military actions was in doubt. In the case of Harmon V. Brucker,[38] the Supreme Court upheld the lower court's assertion of jurisdiction, and quoting Army Regulation 615-360, par. 7, added:

Because the type of discharge may significantly influence the individual's civilian rights and eligibility for benefits provided by law, it is essential that all pertinent factors be considered so that the type of discharge will reflect accurately the nature of service rendered . . .[39]

With this decision, the Court established civil jurisdiction to review military discharges, but for various reasons such review actions have been few and far between. The military has retained relative control of most areas involving service matters and most assuredly in areas dealing with homosexuality.

Even after jurisdiction of the courts had been established, it was assumed that most constitutional safeguards were simply unavailable to military personnel of whatever sexual orientation. In *Beard* v. *Stahr*,[40] the court upheld a statute that placed the burden of proof on the defendant in discharge proceedings and did not provide for confrontation of witnesses. In denying Beard's motion for a preliminary injunction, the court said:

Armies cannot be maintained and commanded, and wars cannot be won by the judicial process. Supervision and control over the selection, appointment and dismissal of officers are not judicial functions. Dismissals of officers are not limited or controlled by the Bill of Rights.[41]

Courts showed themselves particularly reluctant to intervene in military proceedings before all administrative actions and appeals were completed. The courts required a plaintiff to "exhaust all administrative remedies" before entertaining jurisdiction of the case. The harsh reality of this policy was that discharged personnel were often required to spend years in futile administrative appeals before presenting their cases to unsympathetic courts. But an important breakthrough occurred in 1964 with the decision in *Covington* v. *Schwartz.*[42] *Covington* established criteria to determine whether a plaintiff should be awarded a stay of discharge or injunctive relief while the case is pending before military authorities. Plaintiff in *Covington* had completed 16 years of service with an Honorable Discharge, and had re-enlisted for a term of six years as a Sergeant First Class in April of 1961. In 1962, an investigation was commenced. After a year of inquiry by various boards, plaintiff was found to be "homosexual" within the meaning of Army regulations and was recommended for Undesirable Discharge. The court granted plaintiff's motion for a stay of discharge proceedings until he had proceeded through all administrative remedies. The case established four requirements by which to judge a request for a stay of discharge. In order to obtain relief, the plaintiff is required to:

1. establish a likelihood that he or she will prevail on the merits of the appeal,
2. show irreparable harm unless relief is granted,
3. show no harm to other interested persons, and
4. show no harm to the general public.

Covington does not modify the doctrine of exhaustion of administrative remedies, but holds that, in appropriate circumstances, an accused can require that he or she be retained by the service until completion of the administrative review process.

In a few cases, plaintiffs have convinced a court that they should not be required to exhaust administrative remedies before judicial intervention, because of the futility in seeking meaningful administrative review.[43] Plaintiffs have argued that once homosexuality is established, service regulations require dismissal: so, if an accused is not challenging the finding of homosexuality, it is futile to require appeals within the military administrative system. Government response to this argument has been inconsistent and perplexing.

In *Champagne and Stout* v. *Schlesinger* [44] the Navy denied that dismissal of homosexual personnel was mandatory, and averred that from time to time homosexual individuals had actually been retained in the service.[45] The Court of Appeals for the Seventh Circuit accepted the Navy's representation and therefore denied plaintiff's contention that an appeal to the Board of Corrections of Military Records would be futile. The court stated that while the policy of the Secretary of the Navy might appear to require the dismissal of all homosexual members, "the primary authority for the interpretation of such regulations lie(s) within the Navy's own appellate system."[46]

However, the contrary conclusion was reached in *Martinez* v. *Brown*.[47] Judge Cecil Poole of the Northern District of California agreed with plaintiff's contention tht exhaustion of administrative remedies would be futile. He noted:

The Government has belatedly argued that in a literal reading of the regulations, only the processing *for discharge is mandatory, and that they encompass further stages in which consideration is given to the individual's suitability for retention. However, although afforded an opportunity to augment the record to prove that such is the practice, the Government has failed to make any showing in support of such contention.*[48]

Judge Poole therefore construed the regulations to require mandatory discharge.

It is interesting to note the Navy has now deleted from its regulations language concerning mandatory dismissal of homosexual members. Only time will tell if this is a true policy change or only a minor linguistic variation to allow the Navy to argue against discharge stays, as it did in *Champagne and Stout*.

Although there are no specific procedural oddities in the way the services deal with gay people, aside from the exclusion policy itself, such was not always the case. Fannie Clakum was called before her commanding officer in 1951 and interrogated concerning homosexual activities. She was told that she was under investigation but was never informed of any charges ag012inst her. After six months of intensive investigation, she was requested to resign. Clakum refused to do so and demanded a court-martial to present evidence and have charges specifically proven. She was reduced to the rank of Private and discharged pursuant to Air Force Regulation 35-665(b) (1), relating to homosexual personnel. The regulation provided for voluntary resignation with an Undesirable Discharge.

In cases where a service person refused to resign and the evidence indicated that a court martial conviction was unlikely, the Secretary of the Air Force was authorized to direct discharge and determine the nature of the discharge. Clakum brought suit for back pay, charging that dismissal by that method was invalid.[49] Since she denied any homosexual activity, the question of propriety of dismissal on the basis of homosexuality was never reconsidered. Judge Madden stated:

> . . . *it is unthinkable that (the Air Force) should have the raw power, without respect for even the most elementary notions of due process to load her (the plaintiff) down with penalties. It is late in the day to argue that everything that the executives of the armed forces do in connection with the discharge of soldiers is beyond the reach of judicial scrutiny.*[50]

By the time Clakum's case was decided, gay personnel had been accorded procedural protections similar to those enjoyed by all other personnel.[51]

No case in the 1950's and 1960's even alluded to possible constitutional difficulties with the mandatory discharge of gay men and women.[52] In *Crawford* v. *Davis*[53] in 1966, a homosexual soldier sought a preliminary injunction to restrain his impending dismissal. The court denied his motion, finding this would harm the Army.[54] Judge Higgenbottham stated:

> *I think that it would be clearly inappropriate to hobble the Army by forcing it to retain even one soldier for an indefinite period of time, when there are serious questions concerning his emotional health.*[55]

The decision was a natural product of the gratuitous assumption that homosexuality could be equated with serious mental disorders.

The propriety of anti-homosexual military regulations remained unquestioned until the case of *Doe* v. *Chaffee*.[56] In *Doe* v. *Chaffee*, the petitioner asked that he be awarded back pay and an Honorable Discharge in lieu of the Undesirable Discharge he had been given. He did not contest the *authority* of the Navy to discharge him. "Doe" had served nearly four years in the Navy with an excellent record until he admitted an ongoing homosexual relationship with a shipmate. Despite assurances to petitioner that he would be given a General Discharge, he was Undesirably discharged. When subsequently he discovered he was ineligible for veteran's benefits and could not obtain a job in the electronics field, he filed to have his discharged upgraded. Judge Williams summarized the case:

> *(T)he sole question is whether there has been a showing in petitioner's military record of a nexus between his homosexual activity and the quality of his service.*[57]

The requirement of such a connection was not a particularly novel idea. In *Kennedy* v. *Secretary of the Navy*,[58] the court voided the discharge of a Naval officer who had been dismissed for attending Communist party meetings. The court found that a discharge had to be based on activities reflected in the military record and on a finding that the activities affected the quality of service.

What is, perhaps, unique in *Doe* v. *Chaffee* is that the court actually found it necessary to examine the military's justification for dismissal of a homosexual serviceman. Somewhere between *Beard* v. *Stahr* and *Doe* v. *Chaffee* the validity of such dismissals had become less than "self-evident." Nevertheless, Judge Williams found that petitioner's confession of homosexual activity had made the matter part of his military record, and concluded that

(I)t can hardly be argued that the regrettable incident which compelled his early release from the service reflected a performance equal that of millions of other persons who fully carry out their enlistment contracts and receive honorable discharges.[59]

Petitioner's motion was denied.

E. The New Wave: An Enforceable Nexus Requirement?

1. Matlovich and Berg.

Unlike *Doe* v. *Chaffee*, *Matlovich* v. *Secretary of the Air Force*[60] asked the court to reinstate an aggrieved homosexual serviceman. Sergeant Matlovich had compiled a distinguished record of nearly 13 years in the Air Force, including combat duty in Viet Nam, when he decided to inform his superiors of his homosexuality. Matlovich was granted an Honorable Discharge which the Board of Corrections for Military Records refused to set aside. He petitioned to be reinstated, challenging his discharge as unconstitutional.

In August of 1976, Judge Gesell of the District Court of the District of Columbia delivered an oral opinion in which he granted summary judgment to the government. Matlovich had lost what was seemingly a perfect case.

Although Judge Gesell admonished the Air Force for its backward view of homosexuality, and advised a more "discriminatory and informed approach to the problem," he let the regulation stand.

A point which attracted much attention in Gesell's oral opinion was his conclusion that "It is clear, however, from recent cases, that there is no constitutional right to engage in homosexual activity."[61] Judge Gesell was referring to *Doe* v. *Commonwealth's Attorney for the City of Richmond* [62] in which the Supreme Court summarily affirmed the decision of a three-judge district court panel, upholding the constitutionality of Virginia's sodomy statutes.

Even though the Supreme Court itself has questioned whether *Doe* constitutes a carte blanche endorsement of such laws, [63] Judge Gesell reasoned that since prohibitions of homosexual conduct violate no fundamental rights of privacy, such regulations can be sustained on a governmental showing of any rational basis for their existence.

The standard governing judicial review of a discharge from public employment on the ground of homosexuality is, the court believes, one of due process, which requires that the person challenging the government show that there is no rational relation or nexus between the regulations under which the dismissal occurred and any legitimate state interest. [64]

The court accepted the importance of military combat readiness, protection of recruitment, security of military information, and overall efficiency as establishing a legitimate state interest, and concluded that the plaintiff had failed to meet the burden of proof in demonstrating the irrationality of the Air Force regulation. Notably lacking in the decision, however, is any discussion of the *relationship* between the state interest as enunciated and the regulation as constituted or as applied to Matlovich himself. What this means, very simply, is that under due process standards, as seen by Judge Gesell, the government need only show a plausible or vaguely possible rationale for the existence of a statute or regulation to sustain its validity.

Barely nine months later, Judge Gesell was presented with another constitutional challenge to the dismissal of a homosexual officer. In *Berg* v. *Claytor,* [65] the plaintiff challenged his dismissal, claiming his right of privacy had been violated, that the regulation involved was arbitrary and capricious, and that he had been denied a sufficient due process hearing to determine his fitness for retention. Berg's privacy contention was disposed exactly as Matlovich's had been, but in *Berg* the question of requisite nexus between the regulation and legitimate state interests was more thoroughly explored. The Navy suggested that a homosexual officer would be inefficient because enlisted men would not respect him. Berg responded that the record showed that he had had no such problem with subordinates. Nevertheless, the court found the Navy had presented a plausible nexus. The fact that Berg had shown the invalidity of the Navy's hypothesis as applied to him was deemed irrelevant to the question of the regulation's general validity.

Several interesting facts emerge from the discussion in *Berg*. Judge Gesell notes,

The Navy does not argue that it is attempting to maintain moral standards, and it no longer argues that acknowledged homosexuals are security risks.[66]

The sole justification forwarded by the service in *Berg* concerned the inefficiency that would result due to negative reactions of crewmen to a homosexual naval officer. In a footnote the court acknowledged that it is questionable whether such a justification may be legitimately considered. However, the Judge concluded that since homosexual men and women have not yet been found to constitute a "suspect class,"[67] a policy which discriminates against them because of negative reactions of others is perfectly valid. It should, nevertheless, remain a matter of some conjecture whether it is indeed legitimate state policy to perpetuate the bigotry of some citizens for efficiency's sake.[68]

The final matter addressed in *Berg* concerned whether plaintiff was entitled to a due process hearing to determine the specific applicability of the regulations to him. The court said the plaintiff was not entitled to such a hearing because neither his liberty nor property rights had been infringed.[69] A less than honorable discharge would have stigmatized plaintiff, restricting his "liberty," but since Berg was Honorably discharged, the court found no damage to his liberty. Other courts have noted the employment difficulties encountered by those dismissed, even with an Honorable Discharge, who have been accused of homosexual conduct.[70] The Berg court also found the plaintiff had suffered no deprivation of a property interest. The dubiety of the logic used here is readily apparent. Said the court:

Under Navy policy, the Commission of a homosexual act is cause for dismissal. Plaintiff admitted performing homosexual acts, thus he admitted cause for dismissal. Therefore plaintiff had no continued expectation of employment — no property right — and no right to a due process hearing.

The problem with the argument is that it presumes *apriori*, the validity of the naval policy. *Berg* did admit to homosexual acts; he did not admit that they constituted a valid cause for dismissal.

2. Saal/Martinez. Until 1977, all court pronouncements on the ultimate constitutional questions had been negative. But early in 1977

Judge William Schwartzer of the Northern District Court of California ruled that the Navy's blanket exclusion of homosexual persons violated the procedural due process rights of servicewoman Mary Roseann Saal.[71]

Saal had been recommended for general discharge in 1973, but a preliminary injunction was issued to prohibit that discharge pending further proceedings. Just prior to the expiration of her enlistment contract in 1975, the Chief of Naval Personnel denied Saal's request for an extension, ordered her Honorably discharged, but assigned her re-enlistment code RE-4 — ineligible for reinlistment. Saal brought an action to have her application for re-enlistment re-examined, charging she had been denied due process by the Navy's policy of mandatory exclusion of homosexual personnel.

Saal, like Matlovich and Berg, had compiled a very good service record. As in those cases, the judge in *Saal* accepted the contention that homosexual acts are not consitutionally protected. But that is where the parallel ended.

The Navy forwarded a list of justifications for exclusion of homosexuals, including:

1) Tensions and hostilities would exist between known homosexuals and the great majority of naval personnel who despise/detest homosexuality . . . and

2) Homosexuals may be less productive/effective than their heterosexual counterparts . . .[72]

For the first time, a court chose to examine closely the validity of those generalizations. Judge Schwartzer noted that the same grounds could be used to exclude many sorts of people. Undoubtedly, many service people still detest members of social minorities. Disruptive emotional relationships can certainly be engendered by the presence of women in the services. Yet of all social sub-groups, only homosexual persons and those accused of drug trafficking were subject to mandatory dismissal. The problems complained of by the Navy, said the judge, are endemic to heterogeneous society and are usually considered on a case-by-case basis. The fact that the Navy could not possibly contend that the exclusion of all homosexual personnel from the service would eliminate such problems demonstrated the arbitrary nature of the regulations.

While the court's language implies that such regulations are facially invalid, it is important to note that the precise holding of *Saal* is that the Navy regulation is invalid *as applied;* that is, that servicewoman Saal deserved a hearing with respect to her fitness in which the Board was not bound by any mandatory exclusionary policy. In so holding, the court effectively excised all the mandatory language, without actually invalidating the regulation.

One wonders why this should not have been the result in *Berg* also. Judge Gesell found, however, that Berg had not suffered the deprivation of any liberty or property interest and therefore could not argue that he had a right to an individual hearing. *Saal* is squarely at odds with *Berg* on that point. The court in *Saal* recognized that various aspects of the discharge process, even though the discharge was honorable, could have a substantial negative impact on her reputation. The real question in determining whether a liberty interest has been infringed, said Judge Schwartzer, concerns the nature of the charges, and not just the consequences.[73] He found that the charges as reflected in Saal's service record attach a "label of infamy." She was therefore, entitled to a due process hearing.[74]

The effect of *Saal* is to compel the examination of the actual service record of an individual accused of "homosexuality." Homosexuality can be used as a basis for discharge, but only when the record demonstrates it renders the accused "unfit."

Saal was quickly transformed into the beginning of a judicial trend with Judge Cecil Poole's decision in *Martinez* v. *Brown.*[74] The court noted the stigmatizating effect of charges of homosexuality that cause due process rights to attach, and found that

Mandatory exclusion from military service of persons on the basis of homosexual propensity or conduct is irrational and capricious.[75]

The *Martinez* decision seems to go one step beyond *Saal*, in that the court declares the Navy regulation arbitrary and capricious without reference to its application to *Martinez* individually. Thus, the regulation is found to violate *substantive* due process:

. . . due process requires that some nexus be shown between homosexual conduct and unsuitability for service, before a person can be discharged on account of such activity.[76]

The regulation, in providing for a mandatory exclusion by definition, lacked such a requirement. *Martinez* and *Saal* are on consolidated appeal to the Ninth Circuit Court of Appeals.

3. *Matlovich/Berg Revisited.* While gay activists on the West Coast awaited the decision of the Ninth Circuit in *Martinez/Saal,* the *Matlovich*[77] and *Berg*[78] cases proceeded without fanfare to the appellate stage in Washington, D.C.

On December 6, 1978, the U.S. Court of Appeals for the District of

Columbia delivered its opinion in the *Matlovich* and *Berg* cases. The Court vacated the opinion of the lower court in both cases, and remanded the matters for further administrative action.

These decisions were hailed by some as the beginning of a new era. Many gay people within the military presumed that the regulations prohibiting their participation in the Armed Forces had been eliminated by the new decisions. Overlooked in the elation was the fact that Matlovich and Berg had not been restored to their positions. Again the courts had rendered a narrow procedural opinion. The Court in *Matlovich* refused to rule on the broad constitutional challenges to Air Force regulations, saying:

We do not reach these questions because a narrower problem looming before us requires remand of this case to the Air Force, and after further action by the Service renewed consideration by the District Court. [79]

Judge Davis, writing for the Court, emphasized that the Air Force regulations specifically contemplate the possibility of retention of some homosexual personnel.[80] Given that fact, the Air Force was required to explain its reasons for Matlovich's discharge.

We cannot escape the conclusion that the military has itself provided that in cases of this type a reasoned explanation should be made for any detrimental action ordered. [81]

With no explanation on record of the reason for Matlovich's discharge, the Court of Appeal could not tell if the decision had been made in an arbitrary fashion. By way of example, Judge Davis suggested that the military might be retaining only black homosexual personnel, or those who were proteges of senior officers.

The Court strongly urged that the military develop a written policy specifying the circumstances under which gay persons would be retained. Otherwise, such standards would have to evolve on a case by case basis.

The decisions in *Matlovich* and *Berg* do force the Service to enunciate specific reasons for discharge of homosexual personnel, but just how specific those reasons must be, and what sort of criteria will be considered reasonable, were not decided by the D.C. court. Thus, these new decisions are not as far-reaching as *Martinez* and *Saal*. In *Martinez,* for example, the Court rejected the explanation by the Navy that discharge was not mandatory, since the Navy had failed to show any instances where homosexual sailors or officers had been retained. *Martinez* then prescribed unfitness for service as the determinitive factor in discharges.

But the purported discretion to retain gay personnel, accepted by the Court in *Matlovich* and *Berg,* foreclosed decision on such constitutional questions in those cases.[82]

The actual import of the new decisions will not be known for some time. The service regulations now in effect indicate that gay persons will only be retained in exceptional circumstances. Perhaps the Services will eventually adopt the position, recently accepted by the Civil Service, that homosexuality is simply a factor which may be considered but that specific job unfitness must be shown to warrant discharge.

It is also conceivable, however, that the Ninth Circuit will reverse the *Martinez* and *Saal* decisions. That would imply renewed approval of blanket exclusions.

If the attitude of courts in the past is any guide, whatever decision is reached, victory for gay people, if any, will be only procedural.

II. THE HOMOSEXUAL INDIVIDUAL AND NATIONAL SECURITY CLEARANCES

A. Genesis of the Security Clearance Program

No centralized program to protect the security of classified information existed in the United States until shortly after the Second World War, when the Personnel Security Board was created pursuant to an agreement among the branches of the armed services.[83] Prior to that time, individual arms of the military had administered their own security programs.[84] In 1949, the Industrial Employment Review Board was chartered by the secretaries of the armed forces, and a formalized security clearance program began in earnest.[85] Only four years later, the Secretary of the Department of Defense reorganized the security system, establishing regional Industrial Personnel Security Boards and directing the development of uniform standards and criteria.[86]

The form of the present security clearance system resembles that established in 1953 only in its use of regional review boards. In 1960, the procedures of the system were revamped pursuant to a major Supreme Court decision. In *Greene* v. *McElroy,*[87] the Supreme Court held that the Department of Defense had no authority to create a security review system that did not respect minimum due process standards. The *Greene* case provides a good example of the functioning of those early boards. Greene was never provided with all of the information considered by the boards that had reviewed his application for clearance. He was not informed of the precise findings against him until nearly a year after his final hearing, and then some of the findings related to charges which had never been mentioned during the hearing process.

In response to *Greene,* President Eisenhower issued Executive Order 10865,[88] which directs the Department of Defense and other agencies to prescribe regulations for the safeguarding of classified information. By its terms, the Executive Order applies to information within private industry only, and neither to internal information nor to procedures for safeguarding it. The Order includes a broad range of procedural safeguards, including provisions for written statements of reasons for denial of clearance, the opportunity to be represented by counsel at hearings, and the right to confront adverse witnesses. To implement this Executive Order, the Department of Defense issued Directive 5220.6[89] A central office, Industrial Security Clearance Review (ISCR), and various regional offices were established to administer the program.

The standard for granting of clearances was determined to be whether "to do so is clearly consistent with the national interest." The criteria for judging specific applications for clearance are as follows:

1. The facts, circumstances and conduct vary in implication, degree of seriousness, and significance, depending upon all the factors in a particular case.

2. Therefore, the ultimate determination must be an overall common sense one based upon all the information which properly may be considered under this Directive including, but not limited to, such factors as the following:
a. The seriousness of the facts, circumstances and conduct;
b. The implications, the recency, the motivations, the extent to which the conduct was voluntary and undertaken with knowledge of the circumstances involved;
c. The extent that it can be estimated and is appropriate in a particular case, the probability that the conduct will continue in the future . . .[90]

The Industrial Security Clearance Review program has several administrative components. A "Screening Board" initially reviews questionable applications. The Screening Board also has the power to suspend action and, through the Defense Investigative Service (DIS), conduct investigations concerning an applicant, the applicant's background and acquaintances.[91] An applicant may refuse to cooperate in the process, but the Department of Defense is authorized to suspend all action in such cases.[92] Should a Screening Board determine that it is not "clearly consistent with the national interest" to grant a clearance, it must issue a statement of reasons specifying the facts warranting denial.

An applicant who contests the denial must respond in writing to the decision within 20 days of receipt, and may request reconsideration with or without a formal hearing. A "hearing examiner" is then assigned by ISCR to consider all testimony and documentary evidence relating to the charges. As with Boards of Officers in military proceedings, hearing examiners are not bound by strict evidentiary rules.

Hearing examiners are charged to render decisions consistent with the national interest. An examiner's decision must specify the findings and grounds for the decision. Either side may appeal the decision to the Appeal Board in Washington, D.C. This board does not consider any new evidence; it can only review the evidence and decision as prepared by the hearing examiner. However, the board can remand the case to the examiner for further evidence. A decision on the merits by the Appeal Board is final within the administrative process.

B. Homosexuality: Security Risk?

DOD Directive 5220.6 includes fourteen "criteria" for finding ineligibility for clearances. They are meant to be illustrative only and include such expected items as: sabotage, disclosure of classified information, and acts in the interest of a foreign government. Under these criteria, homosexual men and women have routinely been denied clearances or have had their existing clearances revoked.[93] The criteria that are customarily cited to justify such denials are:

H. Any criminal or dishonest conduct, or sexual perversion.

I. Facts, circumstances or conduct of a reckless nature indicating poor judgment, unreliability or untrustworthiness as to suggest that the applicant might fail to safeguard classified information or might disclose classified information to unauthorized persons deliberately or inadvertently. . .

K. Any facts or circumstances which furnish reason to believe that the applicant may be subjected to coercion, influence, or pressure which may be likely to cause action contrary to the national interest. Such facts or circumstances may include the presence of a close relative, friend or associate in a nation whose interests may be inimical to the interests of the United States, or in satellites or occupied areas of such a nation. Close relatives include parents, brothers, sisters, offspring and spouse.[94]

It has long been assumed by the Department of Defense that gay persons are inherently security risks — as is also reflected in the attitude toward homosexual personnel in the military. It is, perhaps, reasonable to assume that an individual who is secretive about this preference might present some security risk, but probably no more than the heterosexual person who engages in covert extramarital sexual conduct. Yet in 1972 the Director of ISCRO, who had been in that agency for nearly 20 years, testified that,

. . . it was conceivable that an ongoing homosexual might be granted a security clearance, but that he could not think of a single case where it had been granted.[95]

Even homosexual individuals who had no fears about blackmail and had demonstrated a record of stability and integrity could be denied a clearance on the basis of criterion H — "sexual perversion." Still, what we are considering here is not an explicit mandatory exclusion of gay persons, as with the military, but a total *de facto* exclusion in force for a period of twenty years.

C. The Nexus Requirement

One of the first cases to test the validity of this system with respect to gay persons was *Adams* v. *Laird*.[96] Adams' homosexuality was discovered when he applied to have his secret level clearance upgraded to top secret. His application was denied and his existing clearance revoked. He maintained that the enunciated standard for denial of clearances was not specific enough to survive due process scrutiny and urged that the government be required to demonstrate the likelihood of abuse of a clearance by an individual applicant to justify denial. The court replied:

We know of no constitutional requirement that the President must, in seeking to safeguard the integrity of classified information, provide that a security clearance must be granted unless it be affirmatively proven that the applicant would use it improperly.[97]

Specifically referring to homosexual applicants, Judge McGowan found:

DOD 5220.6 sets forth many "Criteria," which include ample indications that a practicing homosexual may pose serious problems for the Defense Department in making the requisite finding for security clearance. They refer expressly to the factors of emotional instability and possible subjection to sinister pressures and influences which have traditionally been the lot of homosexuals living in what is for better or worse, a society still strongly oriented towards heterosexuality.[98]

As in the military cases, the court in *Adams* had accepted the inherent validity of government anti-homosexual regulations without requiring proof. However, the parallel with early decisions in the military area comes to an abrupt halt with the 1971 case of *Grimm* v. *Laird*.[99] Grimm's homosexuality came to light when an *unsuccessful* blackmailer reported him to the FBI. Despite his demonstrated reliability, Grimm's clearance was suspended. The District Court of Appeals remanded the case to ISCRO stating:

The Central Board's findings and determination violated due process in that no sufficient rational nexus was shown between plaintiff's homosexual conduct

*and the determination that granting him access to classified defense material is
not clearly consistent with the national interest.*[100]

The nature of the nexus requirement was re-examined in *Wentworth
v. Schlesinger.*[101] Wentworth's clearance had been revoked on the
ground of sexual perversion. Evidence indicated he had engaged in
homosexual activity several years earlier. The applicant established he
had held clearances for a number of years without incident and that
there had "never been the slightest suggestion Wentworth had violated
regulations." The Court of Appeals affirmed the decision of the lower
court that Wentworth's clearance had been improperly revoked and that
decision was based on grounds unrelated to the nexus issue; but the court
discussed that requirement nevertheless.

*With respect to the sufficiency of proof of a nexus between the conduct involved
and security clearance, Adams does not require, as we construe it, objective or
direct evidence . . . What is required is that every application for clearance
must be considered in its particular factual setting. In Mr. Wentworth's case,
this includes the favorable aspects of his life, and in connection with Criterion S
such circumstances as the extent of public knowledge of his sexual life, and the
absence of any record of unfaithfulness to duty . . . The determination in these
cases of security clearance is a judgmental one based on "over-all common
sense," and is to be explained in such a manner that a reviewing court may be
able to discern whether there is a rational connection between the facts relied
upon and the conclusions drawn.*[102]

Due process standards were most recently discussed in *Fultun v.
Secretary of Defense.*[103] The record upon which Fultun's application for
clearance was denied indicated that:

*In addition to the fact of plaintiff's homosexuality, the only significant facts ad-
duced at hearing are that plaintiff has engaged in group sex or that he generally
meets his sex partners in bars.*[104]

Criterion cited for denial of Fultun's clearance included: criminal conduct, sexual perversion, possibility of coercion, and reckless conduct.
The ISCRO Board of Appeal in Fultun's case focused on his admission
of group sexual activity and violation of state sodomy statutes as demonstrating reckless behavior. Judge Orrick of the District Court for the
Northern District of California did not agree that recklessness had been
shown by these facts:

*The decision by the Appeal Board fails to articulate any such rational con-
nection. It simply recites the facts concerning plaintiff's conduct and, with con-*

siderable elaboration but no explanation, concludes that these facts show that plaintiff's trustworthiness, reliability, and responsibility are in serious doubt, and that he is a target for coercion whose resistance to pressure is doubtful. [105]

The burden of proof seems to have undergone a perceptible shift since *Adams.* Under *Fultun,* government justifications for denial of clearances will be scruitinized for a real demonstration of the applicant's unsuitability to safeguard classified information. This does not mean that homosexual applicants will be granted clearances *ab initio,* or that other convenient rationales may not be invoked by hostile bureaucrats for the purpose of weeding out gay persons. For example, in a case decided in 1974, *McKeand* v. *Laird* [106] the Court of Appeals for the Ninth Circuit upheld denial of McKeand's application for a top secret clearance based on a finding that he had once feared disclosure of his homosexuality. The dissenting opinion by Judge Peckham emphasizes the findings of the trial court that McKeand's willingness to challenge the Department of Defense in public proceedings rebuts inferences of the possibility of coercion. Peckham states:

Of course, any homosexual with a security clearance will fear disclosure — if not to his family and friends, at least to the government — as long as the Department of Defense continues to revoke security clearances on a mere finding of homosexuality. However, the Department of Defense easily can cure the danger to national security allegedly posed by all homosexuals. It can abandon its arbitrary system of revoking security clearances solely on a finding of homosexuality and, thus, end homosexuals' fears that public exposure will cost them their security classifications. [107]

D. What Price Clearance?

Security clearance applicants with any demonstrable homosexual involvement in their background can expect to be put through rigorous, embarrassing interviews and, in many cases, to be embroiled in litigation for years, during which time employment opportunities that are dependent on a clearance will be foreclosed. [108] But even the applicant who ultimately is fortunate enough to be granted a clearance by a Screening Board, or who wins a decision from a hearing examiner, will first have to discuss the most intimate sexual affairs at length to convince the government that granting the application is clearly consistent with the national interest. Applicants for clearance are required to answer a Personnel Security Questionnaire (PSQ), which asks whether the applicant has ever been arrested, what organizations the applicant participates in, etc. When the Screening Board finds reason to doubt the suitability of an applicant, an agent may be assigned to conduct in-depth interviews, or the applicant may be required to submit to written interrogatories.

If there is suspicion of homosexuality, the government will ask whether the applicant has engaged in homosexual acts, what acts, when, how many times, where, and under what circumstances.[109] Refusal to provide answers can result in a suspension of all action on the application. The argument that the government should not be able to condition the granting of security clearances on sacrifice of the applicant's privacy rights has met with little success. Otto Ulrich and Richard Gayer both refused to answer certain questions concerning thneir sexual activities. All action by the Department of Defense on clearance upgrades was terminated, and their existing clearances were suspended. Each sued individually to have the suspensions set aside. The district court in *Gayer* v. *Laird* [110] indicated that since plaintiff was admittedly homosexual, questions about his sexual activity could serve no useful purpose and simply invaded his right of privacy.

The *Gayer, Ulrich* and *Wentworth* cases were consolidated on appeal. The appellate court determined that the government can properly inquire about homosexual acts as long as the inquiry is "relevant and is no more intrusive of an applicant's privacy than is reasonably necessary for a rational judgement . . ."[111] The questions asked of Wentworth were found to be impermissibly intrusive, but those asked of Gayer, including: "Name or describe the sexual acts engaged in with other male(s)," were deemed acceptable.[112] Given the standard enunciated in *Gayer,* it seems clear that the government has the right, at present, to inquire into the nature, frequency, and circumstances, including time and place, of an applicant's homosexual acts.

The *Gayer* holding was affirmed in *Marks* v. *Schlesinger.*[113] Plaintiff Marks had held Secret and Top Secret clearances from 1966-1970. His top secret clearance was terminated when he left the Navy in 1970. In 1971, he applied for a secret level clearance in conjunction with his employment with a government contractor. He was informed by his Screening Board that it would suspend action on his request pending completion of interrogatories concerning his alleged homosexual activities. Marks refused to answer the following questions submitted by interrogatories:

IV

Since your resignation from the Navy in July, 1970, have you engaged in any homosexual act(s) with the aforementioned (Mr. A.)? If your answer is "Yes", name or describe the acts (e.g., mutual masturbation, fellatio, sodomy, etc.); advise approximately how many such acts you have engaged in with him; and specify the states and/or foreign countries in which they occurred.

V

Aside from the aforesaid (Mr. A and Mr. B.), have you engaged in any homosexual sexual act(s) with any other male person(s) at any time during the past ten

138

(10) years? If your answer is "Yes", name or describe the acts; advise the approximate number of such other male persons with whom you have engaged in such acts and their approximate age range; and specify the states and/or foreign countries in which the acts occurred.

VI
If your answer to either Question IV or Question V is "Yes", is it your intention to continue to engage in such acts?

VII
If your answer to Question VI is "No", provide the circumstances of your last such act (i.e., date, place, age of other person involved, etc.).[114]

Marks contended the questions were irrelevant and violated his right of privacy. The court allowed,

There is a right under the First Amendment for a person to keep private the intimate details of his sex life and this right applies to homosexuals as well.[115]

But, the court found the questions asked could bear on Mark's susceptibility to coercion. Therefore, the government's security interest was deemed to outweigh Marks's privacy rights.

Taking *Marks* and *Gayer* together, it seems clear that the government may ask any questions which are not so thoroughly unjustifiable as to be deemed "irrelevant." Privacy considerations are to be subordinated. Nevertheless, one doubts that a court would find the privacy interests of a heterosexual married applicant subordinated to government interests, if such an applicant were questioned about potentially illegal acts of oral copulation with a spouse.

E. Present Status: Security Clearance Operations at the Administrative Level

Only two appellate courts have addressed constitutional challenges to security clearance regulations on homosexuality. In *McKeand* v. *Laird*, the court found that applicant's fears of disclosure satisfied the due process nexus requirement. In *Gayer*, Judge Fahy stated that, expert testimony to the contrary, homosexuality alone constituted sexual perversion under DOD 5220.6.[116] The court specifically reserved judgment on whether a finding of sexual perversion alone would support denial of a clearance. The strong indication was that it would.

With the negative decisions from appellate courts in *McKeand* and *Gayer* one might expect ISCR to continue the *pro forma* denial of applications by gay persons. But there is a growing list of applicants who have been granted clearances despite their homosexual conduct.[117] In the case of Elisha Marsh, the hearing examiner found it clearly consistent with the national interest to grant a clearance even though Marsh had been convicted of public lewd conduct in 1971.[118]

The examiner determined that Marsh had engaged in "sexual perversion," as charged, but found in favor of the applicant on the charges of susceptibility to coercion and reckless conduct, stating that Marsh's disclosures to family and co-workers, plus the publicity attendant on the case, negated any possibility of blackmail.[119]

A case decided September 1, 1978, *In re Eaves,* sheds some light on the present attitude of ISCR toward disqualifying homosexual persons per se. Hearing examiner David Henretta found that the applicant's admission that he picks up men in bars on a weekly or monthly basis satisfied the definition of "sexual perversion." But, stated Henretta:

The fact that the Applicant does engage in homosexual acts and will continue to do so in the future does not per se disqualify him from being granted security clearance under the Directive.[120]

In other words, having established the applicant's homosexuality, the government was required to demonstrate how this could constitute a basis for blackmail, or whether his specific acts demonstrated reckless behavior.

The government's trial attorney in *Eaves* argued that the applicant's admission of sexual conduct at gay baths and failure to use condoms despite knowledge of the risks of venereal disease demonstrated a reckless character.[121]

The hearing examiner in adopting the "common sense" analysis mandated by Directive 5220.6 found this recklessness constituted only a "de minimis risk."

As the nexus requirement evolves at the administrative level, examiners appear more willing to decide applications on the basis of common sense rather than stereotypes and tortured logic. Nevertheless, the denial of clearances to gay persons will continue in some fashion as long as ISCR and DOD believe that homosexual conduct alone can present sufficent justification for intrusive inquiries into applicants' sexual activities, and as long as society at large presumes that homosexual persons are more reckless or likely to betray governmental secrets than their heterosexual counterparts.

CONCLUSION

Perhaps in no other areas of gay rights law has progress been so perceptible as in security clearance and military cases, but victories in these areas have been the cause of much frustration. Favorable decisions have been narrowly crafted and fail to confront ultimate constitutional issues. Most of the cases are decided on procedural grounds. The battles for homosexual personnel in the military and in national security employment still have to be fought on a case-by-case basis. This must remain true until gay people receive statutory or judicial protection as a class.

FOOTNOTES

1. See section ten in John Addington Symonds, *A Problem in Greek Ethics*, 1883; Edward Carpenter, Chapter 5, "Dorian Military Comradeship," in *Intermediate Types Among Primitive Folk*, 2nd Ed., 1969; Thokil Vanggaard, *Phallos*, 1972.

2. Carpenter, Chapter 8, "The Samurai of Japan."

3. The high prestige of homosexuality in the Greek world from about 600 B.C. to 400 A.D. was primarily based on the belief that it fostered courage in battle, as Plutarch's *Lives* and his dialogue "On Love" indicate. Evidence suggests that homosexual relations between warriors were first institutionalized by the warlike Dorians of Sparta and Thebes, and then spread to other Greek communities impressed by the Dorian's military efficiency.

    In Plato's *Symposium*, Phaedrus argues that an army made up entirely of lovers would be formidable enough to "overcome the world." (*Works*, ed. Irwin Edman 1928, pp. 341-2.) Unorthodox as the proposal sounds by present-day American standards, such an army was actually recruited at Thebes and held the rank of the leading fighting force in Greece for a generation or more. This was the famous "Sacred Band," composed exclusively of pairs of lovers. (Plutarch, "Life of Pelopidas," In Plutarch's *Lives*.) Greek military leaders in whose lives homosexuality played a significant part include Alexander the Great, Aristides, Themistocles, Lysander, Pelopidas, Epaminandus, and many others. (Noel Garde, *From Jonathan to Gide*, Nosbook Press, 1964.)

    An attitude strikingly similar to the Greek view existed in Japan from the 13th century to the 19th century. Love affairs between samurai warriors and their squires were regarded as more masculine than heterosexual relations and, hence, more proper to the feudal military ruling class. Part of the high esteem in which homosexual relations were held in pre-Meiji Japan sprang from this heroic tradition. (Saikaku Ihara, *Comrade Loves of the Samurai*, Tuttle, 1972.)

4. This is attested to by the writings of Lucretius, Virgil, Catallus, Horace, Ovid, Juvenal, and Martial. (J.Z. Eglinton, *Greek Love*, 1964, Chapter ii.)

5. Among the list are Louis's uncles, César, Duke of Vendome, and Gaston, Duke of Orléans; his brother, Phillip, Duke of Orleans; Henry, Prince of Conde, and his son, "The Great Condé;" the younger Duke of Vendome, and Louis's great enemy, Prince Eugene of Savoy. (Daniel, Marc. "A Study of Homosexuality in France During the Reigns of Louis XIII and Louis XIV," *One Institute Quarterly*, no. 15, 1961.)

6. *Id.*

7. Indeed, of the four greatest generals of Europe — Alexander the Great, Caesar, Frederick the Great, Napoleon, three were bisexual or homosexual. This circumstance does not seem to have diminished their abilities as leaders nor the enthusiasm with which their notably loyal forces fought for them.

8. In Germany, homosexuality between officers and enlisted men can result in loss of pay if an administrative board finds that there was coercion in the relationship.

In Turkey, people who are found to be homosexual are administratively discharged without adverse disciplinary action.

In Greece, homosexual soldiers are referred to a health committee to determine whether or not they should be separated. Standard for separation would appear to be inability to carry out one's duties.

In Denmark, homosexual individuals are not presently drafted, but can enlist and remain in the service. A new law under consideration would shift the burden to the potential draftee to prove unfitness for military service due to homosexuality.

9. In 1919 there was so much concern over alleged immoral activities around the Newport, Rhode Island Naval Base that the Navy instituted a clandestine "investigation." Under the direction of Lieutenant Erasmus M. Hudson and petty naval officer Ervin Arnold, a special squad was organized. Eventually, the squad came under direct supervision and order of then Assistant Secretary of the Navy, Franklin D. Roosevelt. The investigating squad consisted of young men, some of them mere boys, who were sent into Newport to seek "involvement" with military personnel and to report such men for possible court-martial proceedings. Each of the men in the squad was told to use his own "discretion and judgment" whether to permit "immoral acts" actually to be performed upon them. The Senate subcommittee that eventually investigated the practices was of the opinion that both Josephus Daniels, Secretary of the Navy, and Franklin D. Roosevelt, Assistant Secretary of the Navy, had knowledge of the investigation squad shortly after its creation. It was only after the "vicious and immoral" practices of the squad were brought to the attention of the Senate by various Newport clergymen and by the Providence *Journal*, that the subcommittee was formed which investigated and eventually put an end to such practices. ("Alleged Immoral Conditions at Newport (R.I.) Naval Training Station," Report, U.S. Senate, 67th Congress, 1st Session. Committee on Naval Affairs, Washington D.C. 1921, reprinted in *Government Versus Homosexuals,* Arno Press, New York, New York, 1975.)

10. E.W. Kenworthy, "The Case Against Army Segregation," 275 *Annals of the Am. Academy of Pol. and Social Sci.*, 27 (1951).

11. See generally, the House and Senate debates surrounding S.B. 1641, 1947 in Congressional Record, *Proceedings and Debates of the 80th Congress, Second Session.*

12. See generally, *Hearings Before Subcommittee No. 2 of the House Armed Services regarding H.R. 9832, 10705, 11267, 11711, and 13720,* (1974). There has been no evidence that military men will not respect female supervisors.

13. In *Crawford* v. *Davis* 249 F. Supp. 943, 946-947 (E.D. Penn. 1966) the Army justified its exclusion of openly homosexual soldiers with the following contentions:

(a) that a confessed homosexual would create morale problems if young recruits are exposed to him, (b) that office routine would be disrupted by his continued presence . . . (d) that the plaintiff would not be available for full and complete military assignments.

14. Uniform Code of Military Justice, Article 125, 10 U.S.C.A. §925, August 10, 1956.

15. Riukin, Roberts, *The Rights of Servicemen, an ACLU Handbook,* Boran Publishing Company, New York, New York, 1973, p. 69.

16. Secretary of the Navy Instruction, SECNAV 1900.9, dated April 20, 1964.

17. Secretary of the Navy Instruction, SECNAV 1900.9C, dated January 20, 1978.

18. Under Army Regulation 635-200 (Chapter 14) §14-33 (a) Acts of Misconduct (3)

Homosexual Acts, effective February 1, 1978, such acts are described as "bodily contact between persons of the same sex" or as

any proposal, solicitation, or attempt to perform such an act. Members who have been involved in homosexual acts in an apparent isolated episode stemming solely from im-maturity, curiosity, or intoxication normally will not be processed for discharge because of homosexual acts. (emphasis added)

Under Chapter 13, Separation for Unsuitability; §13-2(d), Policy with respect to homosexuality:

It is HQDA policy that homosexuality is incompatible with military service. A person with homosexual tendencies seriously impairs discipline, good order, morale, and security of a military unit.

§13-4(d) provides for discharges where the military record reflects *preservice* homosexual acts.

19. See, as an example, Secretary of the Navy Instruction, SECNAV 1900.9C, dated January 20, 1978.
20. Williams, Colin J. and Weinberg, Martin S. *Homosexuals and the Military*, Harper and Row, New York, NY, 1971.
    There is also a Class IV classification dealing with pre-service actions, although above it has been included under Class III.
21. 54% of the individuals identified by the military as homosexual personnel were reported by others. 29% made voluntary admissions (*op. cit.* pps. 89-90).
22. Brief for plaintiff, *Hess* v. *Schlesinger,* before the U.S. District Court, Southern Dist. of California (John Vaisey, attorney).
23. Williams and Weinberg, *op. cit.,* p. 105.
24. For a complete survey of administrative procedures and the regulations governing each service branch, see Addlestone and Hewman, *ACLU Practice Manual on Military Discharge Upgrading, American Civil Liberties Union Foundation,* New York, New York, 1975.
25. Concrete figures on the number of persons being discharged for homosexuality from each particular branch seems to be a well-guarded secret and not easily attainable. Estimates range from rather conservative numbers, according to military personnel, to enormous numbers according to others on the outside.
26. "Homosexuals in the Military," 37 Fordham L. Rev. 465 (1969).
27. "Homosexuals in the Military," *op. cit.,* p. 466.
28. Air Force Secretary Thomas Reed, commenting on the Matlovich case, was quoted by United Press international as saying that the presence of homosexual soldiers in the military might "corrupt young recruits." *Newswest,* Los Angeles, California, undated article.
29. Roy Root, Director of Information for the Army Reserves at the Pentagon, in a relatively "enlightened" statement suggested development of a program to rehabilitate homosexual personnel in the military. San Francisco *Chronicle,* June 11, 1976.
30. Task Force on the Administration of Military Justice in the Armed Forces, Volume 1-4, Department of Defense, Nov. 30, 1972, Vol. 1, p. 9.
31. *Nelson* v. *Miller,* 373 F. 2d 474 (3rd Cir. 1967).
32. *Id.* p. 477.
33. *Id.*

34. Everhard, John A., "Problems Involving the Disposition of Homosexuals In the Service," II J.A.G. Bul. 6, Nov. 1960.

35. *Matlovich* v. *Secretary of the Air Force,* Civil Action No. 75-1750, Declaratory and Mandatory Relief, First Amended Complaint, United States District Court for the District of Columbia, 1975.

36. *Beller* v. *Middendorf,* C-75-2747.

37. *Doe* v. *Chaffee,* 355 F. Supp. 112, 113 (N.D. Cal. 173). "Doe," a naval serviceman, was given an undesirable discharge after he revealed an ongoing homosexual relationship with a shipmate. In a sworn statement, he admitted ". . . the tension of being together, especially on cruises, and not being able to do what we wanted was causing too much tension and was nerve racking . . ."

38. *Harmon* v. *Brucker,* 355, U.S. 579 (1957).

39. *Id.* at 583.

40. *Beard* v. *Stahr,* 200 F. Supp. 766 (D.D.C. 1961), dismissed as premature 370 U.S. 41 (1961).

41. *Id.,* p. 773.

42. *Covington* v. *Schwartz,* 230 F. Supp. 249 (N.D. Cal. 1964), modified and affirmed *sub nom Schwartz* v. *Covington,* 341 F. 2d 537 (9th Cir. 1965).

43. As an example, see *Martinez* v. *Brown,* _____ F. Supp. _____ (N.D. Cal. 1978).

44. *Champagne and Stout* v. *Schlesinger* 506 F. 2d 979 (7th Cir. 1974).

45. The policy instructions at issue in *Champagne and Stout* were section 3420220 of the Bureau of Naval Personnel Manual (Bu. Pers. Man.) (32 CFR 730.12, 1973) and its implementation in Secretary of the Navy Instruction (SECNAVINST) 1900.9A Bu. Pers. Man. §3420220(3)(e) provided:

Homosexual acts. Processing for discharge is mandatory. (See SECNAVINST 1900.9 series for controlling policy and additional action required in cases involving homosexuality.)

The policy instruction prescribed in said SECNAVINST 1900.9A provided:

4. Policy. The following policy is prescribed:
a. General. Members involved in homosexuality are military liabilities who cannot be tolerated in a military organization . . . Their prompt separation is essential.

At the very least these regulations must be read to mandate the *processing* of all involved in homosexual acts for discharge.

46. *Champagne and Stout, op. cit.,* p. 984, quoting from *Nelson* v. *Miller,* 373 F. 2d 474, 480 (3rd Cir. 1967).

47. *Martinez* v. *Brown,* _____ F. Supp. _____ (N.D. Cal. 1978).

48. *Id.,* p. 8 of memorandum opinion.

49. *Clakum* v. *U.S.* 296 F. 2d 226 (Ct. Cl. 1960).

50. *Id.,* p. 228

51. It is interesting to note, however, that under Secretary of the Navy Instruction 1900.9C, discharges of homosexual personnel are designated a special interest category for "automatic review by the Secretary of the Navy."

52. The court in *Beard* v. *Stahr* 200 F. Supp. 766, 769 n. 3 (1961) cites the Army's regulation, the importance of which the court terms "self-evident."

53. *Crawford* v. *Davis*, 249 F. Supp. 943 (1966).
54. The court used the same standards set in *Covington* v. *Schwartz* 230 F. Supp. 249 (N.D. Cal. 1964), modified and affirmed *sub nom Schwartz* v. *Covington* 341 F. 2d 537 (9th Cir. 1965).
55. *Crawford* v. *Davis, op. cit.* 947.
56. *Doe* v. *Chaffee*, 355 F. Supp. 112 (N.D. Cal. 1973).
57. *Id.*, p. 114.
58. *Kennedy* v. *Secretary of the Navy*, 401 F. 2d 990 (1968).
59. *Doe* v. *Chaffee, op. cit.* 115.
60. *Matlovich* v. *Secretary of the Air Force*, 13 E.P.D. 6088 (1977).
61. *Id.*
62. *Doe* v. *Commonwealth's Attorney for the City of Richmond*, 403 F. Supp. 1199 (1975) summarily affirmed, 425 U.S. 901 (1976). Many commentaries have discussed the significance of *Doe*. (For a recent brief discussion, see Coleman, Thomas, "The Sex Law Explosion," IV Sexual Law Reptr. 21, 23 (Apr./Jn. 1978). Whether the Supreme Court really meant to invite state regulation of the sexual activities of married as well as unmarried citizens, heterosexual as well as homosexual, is highly questionable in light of earlier "privacy" cases. *Griswold* v. *Connecticut* 381 U.S. 479 (1965), established the privacy right of married couples to use contraceptives; *Eisenstadt* v. *Baird* 405 U.S. 438 (1972), extended that right to unmarried couples. If *Doe* is read to apply only to homosexual persons, major questions remain as to the justification for that distinction.
63. In *Carey* v. *Population Services International* 431 U.S. 678 (1977), Justice Brennan stated in his majority opinion:

We observe that the Court has not definitely answered the difficult question whether and to what extent (right of privacy) prohibits state statutes regulating (private consensual sexual conduct) among adults.

64. *Matlovich, op. cit.*, p. 6089.
65. *Berg* v. *Claytor* C. 76-944 (memorandum opinion, May 27, 1977).
66. *Id.*, p. 46
67. The doctrine of suspect classifications holds that the regulations or statutes which discriminate against a "suspect class" will be strictly scrutinized by courts and must be based on a "compelling state interest" to be valid.
68. The court in *Norton* v. *Macy*, 417 F. 2d 1151 (D.C. Cir. 1969), rejected the notion that efficiency of the civil service was a sufficient justification for a per se rule of disqualification of gay persons.
69. Due process rights are invoked by jeopardy to "life, liberty or property."
70. See the discussion in *Nelson* v. *Miller* 373 F. 2d 474 (3rd Cir. 1967), *supra* this chapter.
71. *Saal* v. *Middendorf* 427 F. Supp. 192 (N. D. Cal. 1977).
72. *Saal, op. cit.*, p. 201, n. 10.
73. *Saal, op. cit.*, 198.
74. *Martinez* v. *Brown*, _____ F. Supp. _____ (N.D. Cal. 1978).
75. *Id.*, p. 9.
76. *Id.*, p. 9.
77. *Matlovich* v. *Secretary of the Air Force*, 18 E.P.D. §8710 (1978).
78. *Berg* v. *Claytor*, 18 E.P.D. §8711 (1978).
79. *Matlovich* v. *Secretary of the Air Force, op. cit.* at 4885.
80. The Naval regulations at issue in *Berg* did not reflect any leeway to retain homo-

sexual sailors and officers. However, the Navy in *Champagne and Stout* v. *Schlesinger* 506 F. 2d 979 (7th Cr. 1974) had interpreted those regulations to contain such discretion. The Navy's regulations were amended in January of 1978 specifically to include the possibility of retention.

81. *Matlovich* v. *Secretary of the Air Force, op. cit.* at 4888.

82. The only suggestions that there may be some inherent infirmity in the service's regulations come in two footnotes to the *Matlovich* opinion. Footnote 9 raises equal protection questions, with the note that "the Air Force stipulated that it does not seek to suppress heterosexual activity, which is technically in violation of the Uniform Code of Military Justice or state laws." Footnote 10 reserves the question of whether it is indeed constitutional "to separate servicemen who engage in private consensual homosexual conduct with adults, off-duty and off-base." The Court of Appeals in *Matlovich*, unlike Judge Gesell below, does not assume that *Doe* v. *Commonwealth's Attorney for the City of Richmond*, 425 U.S. 901 (1976) is dispositive of all privacy questions with regard to homosexual conduct.

83. *Greene* v. *McElroy* 360 U.S. 474, 493-494 (1959).

84. *Id.*

85. *Id.*, p. 478, n. 4.

86. *Id.*, p. 480.

87. *Greene* v. *McElroy*, 360 U.S. 474 (1959).

88. 25 Fed. Reg. 1583 (1960), as amended 3 C.F.R. 512 (1968).

89. 25 Fed. Reg. 14399 (1960).

90. DOD Directive 5220.6, IV F., as reissued December 20, 1976.

91. *Id.*, p. 8.

92. *Id.*, p. 3

93. *Government Created Employment Disabilities of the Homosexual*, 82 Harv. L. Rev. 1738 (1969), and *Security Clearances for Homosexuals*, 25 Stan L. Rev. 403 (1973).

94. D.O.D. Directive 5220.6, *op. cit.*, pp. 5-6.

95. *Wentworth* v. *Laird*, 348 F. Supp. 1153, 1155 (1972).

96. *Adams* v. *Laird* 429 F. 2d 230 (D.D.C. 1961), *cert. denied*, 397 U.S. 1039 (1970).

97. *Id* at 239.

98. *Id.*

99. *Grimm* v. *Laird*, Civil No. 173-71, unpublished opinion (D.D.C. 1971).

100. *Id.*

101. The *Wentworth* case was consolidated with two others on appeal and appears *sub nom Gayer* v. *Schlesinger* 490 F. 2nd 740 (1973).

102. *Id.* at 750-751.

103. *Fultun* v. *Secretary of Defense*, unpublished (N.D. Cal. 1978).

104. *Id.* at 3.

105. *Id.* at 4.

106. *McKeard* v. *Laird* 490 F. 2d 1262 (1973).

107. *Id.* at 1265-1266.

108. For example, in the *Fultun* case, Fultun's application for a secret clearance was denied in 1974. The decision in *Fultun* v. *Secretary of Defense* finds the rationale for denial of Fultun's clearance was improper, but Judge Orrick refused to order that Fultun's clearance be granted. The case has been remanded to ISCR, and still continues five years after it began.

109. *See Gayer* v. *Schlesinger* 490 F. 2d 740 (1973) for examples of questions asked.

110. *Gayer* v. *Laird* 332 F. Supp. 169 (1971), reversed and remanded *sub nom Gayer* v. *Schlesinger* 490 F. 2d 740 (1973).

111. *Gayer* v. *Schlesinger, op. cit.*, p. 754.

112. The questions taken from *Gayer* v. *Schlesinger* 490 F. 2d 470 (1973), J. Robb, concurring in part, dissenting in part at 756, include:

II. Have you ever engaged in any homosexual act(s) or any act(s) of sexual perversion with (an) other male person(s)?

III. (If the answer to Question II is "Yes", answer the following):
1. Name or describe the sexual acts engaged in with other male(s):
2. Approximately how many such acts have occurred?
3. Dates (approximate) or the period within which such acts have been engaged in:
4. Where were such acts performed?
5. What were the circumstances leading to the last such act? (Be specific as to where, when. . . the act was performed.)

113. *Marks* v. *Schlesinger* 384 F. Supp. 1373 (C.D. Cal. 1974).
114. *Id.*, p. 1376.
115. *Id.*
116. *Gayer* v. *Schlesinger, op. cit.*, p. 748
117. The list includes Otis Tabler, who received a favorable determination from Examiner Richard Farr in 1974; Elisha Marsh, who was granted a clearance in 1976; and John Napier Eaves in 1978.
118. The Examiner *In re Marsh*, OSD 74-199, May 3, 1976, emphasized that Marsh's illegal conduct had not been repeated, and that he was unlikely to engage in such conduct again since the applicant "now is familiar with the homosexual community, to the extent that he no longer would find such a risky undertaking necessary in order to make contact with other homosexuals." (at p. 8.)
119. A common defense tactic in these cases is to invite as much public attention and media coverage as possible. The theory is that this will prove the applicant does not fear disclosure of homosexuality.
120. *In re Eaves,* OSD 77-466, p. 17 (1978).
121. "Post-Hearing Brief" by Government's Trial Attorney, *In re Eaves,* p. 15.

THE EMERGENCE OF ASSOCIATIONAL RIGHTS FOR HOMOSEXUAL PERSONS

Donald M. Solomon, J.D.

In law, as in many other fields of social policy, the process by which decisions are reached is often as significant as the decisions themselves. This article seeks to use a series of judicial opinions in one area of constitutional law to illustrate the development over the years of a judicial attitude toward homosexuality.

I. HOMOSEXUAL ASSOCIATION: TRENDS OF DECISION

The First Amendment to the United States Constitution includes a number of conceptually distinct individual rights: the protection of the free exercise of religion; the prohibition of established churches; protection of the freedoms of speech and press; and "the right of the people peaceably to assemble, and to petition the Government for a redress of grievances." All of these guarantees, of course, affect gay persons, but few of the rights have received substantial attention by the courts in that context. In order to illustrate the law's response to homosexuality, this article will concentrate on the right of association under the First Amendment.[1]

The right of association—the right to join and be identified with other persons for common goals—has developed as an amalgam of the freedoms of speech and assembly. For example, it has been held in a long line of cases that membership in political organizations cannot be made unlawful unless that membership is specifically intended to further an unlawful purpose, such as the overthrow of the government.[2] Any association with a "first amendment" component—that is, association for the purpose of political activity, oratory, or publication—is thus protected under the Constitution. Association for its own sake (as, for example, in a domestic relationship) cannot find protection in the First Amendment

---

Donald M. Solomon is a member of the California and Connecticut bars. He earned his B.A. at Brooklyn College and his J.D. at Harvard Law School.

but must look to other constitutional provisions. The Supreme Court held in *Healy* v. *James*[3] that a university must grant campus recognition to the Students for a Democratic Society (SDS) on the same terms as other groups, because the university could not prove that SDS was likely to cause disruption. However, in a case where a local zoning ordinance forbade three or more unrelated persons to live together, the Court held that the right of association was irrelevant.[4] The traditionally broad zoning power prevailed, in part because the group had assembled not for agitation but for habitation. It appears that if unrelated persons have any constitutional right to live together, that right does not stem from the First Amendment right of association and consequently does not enjoy the same "preferred position" that the court has traditionally reserved for First Amendment rights.[5]

Applying these principles to homosexual persons has been a perplexing problem for many courts, because the courts see the principal claim of gay organizations as arising out of sexual conduct, which is not protected by the First Amendment. This attitude is illustrated by *State ex. rel. Grant* v. *Brown*,[6] in which the Greater Cincinnati Gay Society was denied permission to file articles of incorporation. In a terse opinion, the Supreme Court of Ohio declared that "the promotion of homosexuality as a valid lifestyle is contrary to the public policy of the state." This being so, the purposes of the society were not lawful and it could not be allowed to incorporate. In *Mississippi Gay Alliance* v. *Goudelock*,[7] a federal appeals court held that a college newspaper could not be compelled to accept an advertisement for an association providing counseling, legal aid, and social activities for homosexual men and women. Among other holdings, the court opined that to form an association, in and of itself, would lead the members of the Gay Alliance to violate Mississippi's sodomy laws.

Judicial recognition of homosexual people's associational rights found its first expression in cases involving gay bars — practically the only form of social organization open to homosexual men and women until the 1960's. In those cases, the Supreme Court of California held that a liquor license could not be revoked solely because the premises were "a resort for sexual perverts." The court held simply and directly that homosexual adults have the right to congregate in bars and restaurants for lawful purposes, just as does any other segment of society.[8] A contrary attitude is illustrated by a recent Florida decision, *Inman* v. *City of Miami*,[9] in which the court held that the state had a legitimate reason to "prevent the congregation at liquor establishments of persons likely to prey upon the public by attempting to recruit other persons for acts which have been declared illegal . . ."

The attitude of the Florida District Court of Appeal in *Inman* is rapidly fading, though it has by no means vanished. After the Supreme Court ruling in *Healy* v. *James* that the First Amendment protects even such radical organizations as SDS, many gay students' groups sought similar recognition at other colleges. Most were successful. In *Gay Students Organization* v. *Bonner*,[10] the United States Court of Appeals for the First Circuit candidly phrased the question before it as

whether, whatever may be Supreme Court precedent in the First Amendment area, group activity promoting values so far beyond the pale of the wider community's values is also beyond the boundaries of the First Amendment, at least to the extent that university facilities may not be used by the group to flaunt its credo.

Noting that the Gay Students Organization was not organized to incite or engage in illegal conduct, the court found itself "unable to devise a tolerable standard exempting this case at the threshold from general First Amendment precedents."[11] This marks perhaps the first instance where a federal appeals court has explicitly decided that the activity of homosexual men and women in meeting together in order to discuss homosexuality is at least presumptively protected by the Constitution. Having come that far, it was relatively easy for the court to conclude on the record before it that the university's speculation about possible criminal acts or other anti-social conduct was merely "undifferentiated fear," masking concerns undeserving of judicial consideration.

Other court decisions involving student organizations have reached similar results. In *Gay Alliance of Students* v. *Matthews*,[12] the Fourth Circuit Court of Appeals rejected the reasons tendered by Virginia Commonwealth University for denying recognition. The court held that the university could not bar recognition of such a group as a means of discouraging membership or preventing homosexual individuals

from meeting one another to discuss their common problems or possible solutions to those problems . . . Individuals of whatever sexual persuasion have the fundamental right to meet, discuss current problems, and to advocate changes in the status quo, *so long as there is no "incitement to imminent lawless action."*

The university could attempt to discourage homosexual conduct, but "denial of registration is overkill."

The wave of litigation on this issue spread to Missouri, where a group called Gay Lib requested recognition from the University of Missouri. Unlike the other institutions which denied such requests summarily, here the university appointed an attorney as a hearing officer and directed him to hold a hearing on the application. After considerable testimony was given, the hearing officer rendered "findings of fact" in which he concluded that, unless Gay Lib's members made a concerted effort to seek medical treatment, university recognition of the group would

perpetuate and expand an abnormal way of life . . . (and) tend to expand homosexual behavior which will cause increased violations of (Missouri's sodomy law). . .[13]

When the group sought federal court review of the university's action, the trial court upheld the university, in part on the basis of testimony by Dr. Charles Socarides that "wherever you have a convocation of homosexuals, . . . you are going to have increased homosexual activities which, of course, includes sodomy."[14] The court then held that the university had the right to refuse recognition to the Gay Lib group "where the result predictably is to bring on the commission of crimes against the sodomy statutes of the State of Missouri."[15] On appeal, the Court of Appeals for the Eighth Circuit found that the evidence presented by Socarides and others was "insufficient to justify a governmental prior restraint on the right of a group of students to associate for the purposes avowed in their statement . . . (;) restrictions on First Amendment rights in the present context may be justified only by a far greater showing of a likelihood of imminent lawless action than that presented here."[16]

The Missouri case did not end in the Court of Appeals. The university filed a petition for *certiorari* in the United States Supreme Court, which summarily denied the petition, as it does in thousands of cases each year. Justices Rehnquist and Blackmun filed a dissenting opinion, in which they suggested that the university's action was justified as an attempt by the state "to prevent the subversion of the lawful rules of conduct which it has enacted pursuant to its police power . . ."[17] Without expressly endorsing the views of the university, these Justices asserted that the views were entitled to great and perhaps decisive weight in this case. Justice Rehnquist characterized the university's position as

akin to whether those suffering from measles have a constitutional right, in violation of quarantine regulations, to associate together and with others who do not presently have measles, in order to urge repeal of a state law providing that measle sufferers be quarantined. The very act of assemblage under these circumstances undercuts a significant interest of the State. . .[18]

This is a rather emotional and provocative way of stating the case against recognizing the Gay Lib group. Although Justice Rehnquist apparently devised the analogy himself, he presented it not as his own view but as a restatement of the university's position, which he was not "free to reject."

II. COMMENTS ON THE DECISIONAL PROCESS

The *Gay Lib* case illustrates the tendency of some courts to hide behind the "factual findings" of other lower courts or administrative agencies, even when those findings are obviously without foundation. Courts frequently defer to the decisions of others as a matter of governmental policy. For example, in theory a court cannot reexamine facts which were determined in a prior court decision between the same parties. The power to decide disputes is delegated to administrative agencies, and an agency's decision will not be overturned by a court unless it appears clear that the judgment is

(not) justified by a fair estimate of the worth of the testimony of witnesses or its informed judgment on matters within its special competence or both. [19]

The courts go further and abstain from decision altogether to preserve the balance of powers among the branches of government. Under our Federal system, federal courts cannot enjoin pending criminal actions in state courts, even where constitutional questions are raised. [20] Courts treat as "political," and refuse to decide, those few questions which are constitutionally committed to the final authority of the executive or legislative branches of government and those questions for which "judicially manageable" criteria of decision are lacking. [21] Appellate courts frequently limit themselves to "questions of law," reviewing the factual determinations of trial courts only if the supporting evidence is so sparse as to suggest that the decision was irresponsible, not merely wrong.

In times of controversy and change, this rule of deference has been used by the judiciary to avoid their responsibility to decide the cases that come before them. The precise motives for this avoidance are debatable — they may represent a desire to allow public pressure and the "political branches" of government to hammer out the issues at greater length, or an unprincipled failure to explicate what is in fact an agreement with one side of a controversial issue. For example, the Supreme Court consistently rejected the several invitations to decide the constitutionality of the Vietnam War. [22] During the last few wars, the decisions of draft boards were given the widest possible deference, even when clearly erroneous, lest the courts become "super draft boards." [23] Procedural rules, such as those governing "standing to sue" and mootness, have been employed to postpone decisions involving affirmative action, contraception, and religion.[24] Perhaps the greatest extent of this deference occurred during the Cold War, when the Court refused to reexamine "findings of fact" made, not by a court but by Congress, on the existence and dangerousness of a so-called "world Communist movement."[25]

In addition to these articulated rules, the United States Supreme Court enjoys absolute discretion to accept or reject petitions for *certiorari*, the most commonly used method of obtaining review. The Court also employs a variety of devices to dispose of the appeals "as of right" that it does not wish to hear. In effect, the Court can choose which current issues it will resolve and which it will not. The most celebrated "non-decisions" in recent years have concerned interracial marriage and consensual homosexual acts.[26]

The *Inman* decision, upholding state laws which forbade homosexual people to gather in bars, gives the policymaking branch of government a degree of latitude that is out of place where civil liberties are implicated. The district court in *Gay Lib*, and Mr. Justice Rehnquist in his dissent in the case, rely heavily on a principle of deference to the decisions of administrative agencies. However, the "administrative decision" in *Gay Lib* was not that of an established agency with a clearly defined jurisdiction upon which to base a claim of special expertise. It was, rather, the result of an an *ad hoc* hearing held by an attorney with no special knowledge of campus affairs or of homosexuality. The "decision" deferred to in *Gay Lib* was not a finding of fact based on the evaluation of eyewitness testimony but simply a manifestation of agreement with one psychiatrist's theory of homosexuality. There is no logical reason or public policy that explains why that sort of conclusion should be immune from judicial scrutiny, and the Eighth Circuit properly elected to reexamine it. It is ironic that this exercise in judicial activism prompted Justice Rehnquist to criticize the Supreme Court's refusal to review as "a sort of judicial storm cellar to which we may flee to escape from controversial or sensitive cases,"[27] for it is exactly that sort of avoidance technique which the district court had employed earlier and which Justice Rehnquist would have voted to affirm.

The Rehnquist view of the *Gay Lib* case may be characterized as unprincipled in the sense that it would employ judicial deference not simply to postpone the resolution of a politically charged question, but to mask a substantive agreement with an illiberal theory of homosexuality that the present Court is unwilling or unable to justify.

When the substantive issues implicate only economic relationships, the courts' reluctance to interfere with administrative decisions or legislative policy judgments may be justified. But deferring to an administrative agency in its efforts to fix complicated railroad rate schedules[28] is far different from leaving the grant or denial of a parade permit to the unfettered "administrative" discretion of the local police chief.[29] As Archibald Cox has said:

To apply the philosophy of judicial self-restraint to the area of speech and press would entrust those liberties to the substantially uncontrolled power of the individual states and the Congress. In the historical context the very presence of the Bill of Rights in the Constitution implies that its framers intended to provide restrictions upon legislative power over certain areas of human activity in which liberty was deemed especially important.[30]

To characterize substantive value judgments about the relative importance of free speech and conventional morality as unreviewable administrative "decisions" is not only to abdicate the Court's role as the supreme constitutional arbiter; it is to allow the Court to make constitutional decisions from behind an intellectual screen.

III. CONCLUSION

Court decisions involving the right of homosexual persons to meet together for social and political purposes have begun to acknowledge that such associations are constitutionally protected to some extent. The earlier judicial attitude was exemplified by decisions deferring to the judgment of other governmental entities. In addition to frustrating the development of the law and giving too little weight to civil liberties, these decisions reflected the view that gay people are purely sexual beings whose inevitable tendency is to violate the criminal law and the state's social policies. At this writing, the trend of decisions seems to favor recognizing homosexual persons as capable of associating together independently of their sexual lives. That recognition is essential to developing the concept of homosexual persons as a class worthy to enjoy constitutional protections.

FOOTNOTES

1. Another area in which homosexuality has been litigated in the context of the First Amendment is that of obscenity and pronography. See, e.g., *Mishkin* v. *New York,* 383 U.S. 502 (1966); *Manual Enterprises* v. *Day,* 370 U.S. 478 (1962); *One, Inc.* v. *Olesen,* 241 F. 2d 772 (9th Cir. 1957). That area offers limited possibilities for analysis because obscenity is not constitutionally protected, and because pornographic documents sold to homosexual audiences may not be published by homosexual persons at all. In reviewing the constitutional rights of gay persons, it is necessary to focus on controversies that involve homosexual men and women as the speakers or writers, no matter what the content of the speech or the nature of the audience.

2. *NAACP* v. *Alabama ex. rel. Patterson,* 357 U.S. 449 (1958); *Noto* v. *United States,* 367 U.S. 290 (1961); *Baird* v. *State Bar,* 401 U.S. 1 (1971); *In re Stolar,* 401 U.S. 23 (1971). These cases held, in a variety of contexts, that individuals could not be penalized, directly or indirectly, for membership in any organization unless the group itself had an unlawful aim which the individual specifically intended to further by joining it.

3. *Healy* v. *James,* 408 U.S. 169 (1972).

4. *Village of Belle Terre* v. *Boraas,* 416 U.S. 1 (1974).

5. "[F]reedom of thought, or speech . . . is the matrix, the indispensable condition, of nearly every other form of freedom." *Palko* v. *Connecticut,* 302 U.S. 319 (1937). *See New York Times Co.* v. *United States,* 403 U.S. 713 (1971) (the Pentagon Papers case).

6. *State ex. rel. Grant* v. *Brown,* 39 Ohio St. 2d 112, 313 N.E. 2d 842 (1974). *Compare Gay Activists Alliance* v. *Lomenzo,* 31 N.Y. 2d 965, 293 N.E. 2d 255, 341 N.Y.S. 2d 108 (1973) (allowing incorporation whenever the technical requirements are met).

7. *Mississippi Gay Alliance* v. *Goudelock,* 536 F. 2d 1073 (5th Cir. 1976), *cert. denied,* 97 S. Ct. 1678 (1977).

8. *Stoumen* v. *Reilly,* 37 Cal. 2d 713, 234 P. 2d 969 (1951); *Vallerga* v. *Department of Alcoholic Bev. Control,* 53 Cal. 2d 313, 347 P. 2d 909, 1 Cal. Rptr. 494 (1959).

9. *Inman* v. *City of Miami,* 197 So. 2d 50 (Fla. App. 1967).

10. *Gay Students Organization* v. *Bonner,* 509 F. 2d 652 (1st Cir. 1974).

11. *Ibid.* at 658.

12. *Gay Alliance of Students* v. *Matthews,* 544 F. 2d 162 (4th Cir. 1976).

13. *Gay Lib* v. *University of Missouri,* 416 F. Supp. 1350, 1358 (W.D. Mo. 1976).

14. *Ibid.* at 1369.

15. *Ibid.* at 1370.

16. *Gay Lib.* v. *University of Missouri,* 558 F. 2d 848 (8th Cir. 1977).

17. *Ratchford* v. *Gay Lib,* 434 U.S. 1080, 98 S. Ct. 1276, 1278 (1978).

18. *Ibid.* at 1084. Other cases involving the right of association of gay persons are *Toward a Gayer Bicentennial Committee* v. *Rhode Island Bicentennial Fdn.,* 417 F. Supp. 632 (D.R.I. 1976) (recognition of gay group by bicentennial commission); *Wood* v. *Davison,* 351 F. Supp. 543 (N.D. Ga. 1972) (student group).

19. *Universal Camera Corp.* v. *National Labor Relations Board,* 340 U.S. 474, 490 (1951).

20. *Hicks* v. *Miranda,* 422 U.S. 332 (1975); *Younger* v. *Harris,* 401 U.S. 37 (1971); *see Douglas* v. *City of Jeannette,* 319 U.S. 157 (1943); *Schlesinger* v. *Councilman,* 420 U.S. 738 (1975), applied the rule to pending courts - martial.

21. *Baker* v. *Carr,* 369 U.S. 186 (1962).

22. *See, e.g., Massachusetts* v. *Laird,* 400 U.S. 886 (1970). One case that reached the issue concluded that Congress had validly declared war. *Orlando* v. *Laird,* 443 F. 2d 1039 (2d Cir. 1971).

23. *Witmer* v. *United States,* 348 U.S. 375, 380-81 (1953).

24. *See De Funis* v. *Odegaard,* 416 U.S. 312 (1974) (affirmative action); *Tileston* v. *Ullman,* 318 U.S. 44 (1943) (contraception); *Poe* v. *Ullman,* 367 U.S. 497 (1961) (same) *Doremus* v. *Board of Educ.,* 342 U.S. 429 (1952) (Bible reading in public schools). Those questions were later decided in *Regents of the Univ. of Calif.* v. *Bakke,* 438 U.S. —, 98 S. Ct. 2733 (1978); *Griswold* v. *Connecticut,* 381 U.S. 479 (1965); *Abingdon School Dist.* v. *Schempp,* 374 U.S. 203 (1963), respectively.

25. *Communist Party* v. *Subversive Activities Control Bd.,* 367 U.S. 1, 94-95 (1961). The Court also relied heavily on the Control Board's findings that the American Communist Party was dominated by the Soviet Union. *Ibid.,* at 54-55. The Court was therefore able to sustain an order requiring the Party to register as a subversive organization without any judicial evaluation of the evidence supporting the order.

26. *See Naim* v. *Naim,* 350 U.S. 891 (1955), *on remand,* 197 Va. 734, 90 S.E. 2d 849, *motion denied,* 350 U.S. 985 (1956) (interracial marriage); *Doe* v. *Commonwealth's Attorney,* 425 U.S. 901 (1976) (consensual homosexual acts). Interracial marriage was finally given constitutional protection in *Loving* v. *Virginia,* 388 U.S. 1 (1967).

27. *Ratchford* v. *Gay Lib,* 434 U.S. 1080, 1081 (1978).

28. *Railroad Commission of Texas* v. *Pullman Co.,* 312 U.S. 496 (1941).

29. *See, e.g., Thomas* v. *Collins,* 323 U.S. 516 (1945); *Lovell* v. *Griffin,* 303 U.S. 444 (1938); *Niemotko* v. *Maryland,* 340 U.S. 268 (1951).

30. A. Cox, *The Role of the Supreme Court in American Government* 50-51 (1976). The line between economic regulation and free speech is not always a clear one. In *Council on Religion and the Homosexual* v. *Pacific Tel. & Tel. Co.,* 70 Cal. P.U.C. 471 (1969), the Public Utilities Commission — itself an administrative agency — sustained the telephone company's refusal to provide a classified directory heading for "homophile organizations." The Commission applied an extremely deferential standard in reviewing the company's decision, ignoring the underlying civil rights questions. See also *Society for Individual Rights* v. *Pacific Tel. & Tel. Co., 71 Cal.* P.U.C. 622 (1970) (classified advertisement).

The Publishers gratefully acknowledge the aid of Robert L. Buckwalter in the preparation of the Index and Table of Cases for this volume.

DATE DUE

APR 8 1982			
MAR 2 1 1985			
4-21-86			
MAR 27 1990			
FEB 1 7 1993			
NOV 0 9 2010			